False Doctrine and the Wrath of God

Christopher Ricci

PublishAmerica

Baltimore

First printing

Young's Analytical Concordance of the Bible is used by permission of Thomas Nelson Inc.

ISBN: 1-4137-1539-7
PUBLISHED BY PUBLISHAMERICA, LLLP
www.publishamerica.com
Baltimore

Printed in the United States of America

DEDICATION

I would like to extend a special thanks to my beloved wife and best friend, Cynthia, for all her patience, faith, and support in this endeavor. Without her this project would still be incomplete. I would like to thank my good friends, James Clark and Jeffrey Danko. Our conversations around the fireplace led to many of the Truths found in this book. I would also like to thank my uncle Steve and aunt Janet for taking me into their home at a troubled time in my life and introducing me to the Lord. They are two of the finest Christians I've ever known. Above all, I'd like to thank my dear mother Suzanne. She has been a pillar of strength throughout my life. Words cannot describe how grateful I am for all she's done for me. Finally, I would like to thank the Lord God but I don't know how. My heart struggles desperately to utter the unspeakable words within. This is like a foreign language that I completely understand but man has not yet created words for its translation. Only He can know how eternally grateful I am, so I suppose a simple "Thank You" will have to suffice.

Prelude

"I am young:
and ye are very old:
wherefore I was afraid,
and durst not show you mine opinion.
I said, Days should speak,
And multitude of years should teach wisdom.
But there is a spirit in a man:
And the inspiration of the Almighty
Giveth them understanding.
Great men are not always wise:
Neither do the aged understand judgment.
Therefore I said, Hearken to me;
I also will show mine opinion…
For I am full of matter;
The spirit within me constraineth me.
Behold, my belly is as wine which hath no vent;
It is ready to burst like new bottles.
I will speak, that I may be refreshed:
I will open my lips and answer.
Let me not, I pray you, accept any man's person;
Neither let me give flattering titles unto man.
For I know not to give flattering titles;
In so doing my Maker would soon take me away."

(Job 33:6-10, 18-22)

TABLE OF CONTENTS

INTRODUCTION

In writing this I wanted to alert my readers to the very possible dangers of certain important religious ideas, namely, antinomianism, the pretribulation rapture, and the millennium. When I initially began writing this book my intentions were to focus only on the rapture and the millennium. But the more I researched the pretribulation rapture concept the more I realized that I needed to address the issue of antinomianism as well. Antinomianism is the belief that Christians are "saved" by faith and grace alone and therefore they will not be held accountable for their actions no matter what they do (or don't do). And since these people believe they are already destined for the Kingdom of Heaven they see no need for punishment, correction, tribulation, or judgment. But this belief could lead to spiritual complacency, presumptuousness, and self-righteousness, and has been instrumental in the rapture's birth and phenomenal popularity. The rapture concept creates the false hope that Christians will be exempt from upcoming tribulation. This idea is not true. Christians always have been, are now, and always will be subjected to tests, trials, and tribulations. The millennium sets up the perfect stage for the emergence of false christs. These theories are dangerous and contrary to both scripture and Christianity. This book is designed to help my readers better understand these ideas and to make an informed decision as to whether or not they should be accepted as infallible truth.

This is a book of reform and rectification. Hence, it is formidable and very straight forward. But it is not an accumulation of degradations. I've labored painstakingly to remain as noncritical and deferential as possible. I'm certainly not attempting to hurt anyone's feelings. Neither am I attempting to place heavy burdens upon you. I am rather trying to lesson burdens that already exist; but many Christians are not aware of them. I merely want to build upon the sure foundation of truth. It is my sincere hope that this will separate hypothetical speculation from constructive doctrine.

Due to the portentous feeling that I haven't much time before it's too late, I will be as compendious as possible. So if by chance I were to die, or something equally "drastic" were to occur, my views could be made known. There aren't enough words nor paper to write them on which could fully convey my thoughts and feelings about the subjects within this. On the most important ideas I will be very explicit. But I've tried my best to keep the exiguous details to a minimum, for example, my views regarding predestination, the meanings of symbolical prophecy, and current world affairs. I feel I could write a capacious book on each of those topics. But for the present I need to focus primarily upon antinomianism, the pretribulation rapture, and the millennial concepts.

I've included a detailed outline of the entire text at the beginning of the book. This could give my readers a sense of direction and help in locating relevant issues as I address them. Unless indicated otherwise all Biblical quotations employed within this are taken from the King James Version of the Bible and will be *italicized*.

Before I begin, I'd like to remind my readers of one thing: Oftentimes, people read right through certain books without pausing to research the scriptural passages quoted within them. This is precisely how some Christians have been misled by various religious doctrines. So if you are at all skeptical about my use of a particular Biblical quotation, I recommend that you pause briefly, look up the questionable reference, and research the passage contextually. This way you are not following blindly and you can be certain that what I am saying is the truth.

Friends, it is good to read this, and any other book written by man about the Bible, with caution. Since no man is perfect, any book about God, written by a man, is subject to imperfection. Therefore I not only invite you to scrupulously examine the contents of this book, but I absolutely expect it. If you ask the Lord for guidance and wisdom He will not forsake you. I'm not asking you to let your guard down to me or anyone else. But if you are to receive these gifts from the Lord, you must drop your guard to Him. This is especially true for those of you who already accept these theories as fact. So take your time, relax, don't start apprehensively. I'm not standing there right next to you saying these things directly to you. So there's no need to be defensive about this. It's between you and the Lord now.

Whether or not you agree with what I say, I'm certain you will discover much food for thought. All of my ideas are supported with very concrete scriptural evidence. If perchance, you tend to disagree with anything within this, weigh the facts and draw your own conclusions. All I ask is that you try to maintain a reasonably open mind and don't stop reading.

* <u>CONSPECTUS</u> <u>OF</u> <u>CHAPTERS</u> <u>1-14</u> *

<u>CHAPTER</u> <u>ONE</u>: <u>ANTINOMIANISM</u> <u>IN</u> <u>THE</u> <u>CHURCH</u>

- Antinomianism in the Church.
- Some Christians are under the false impression that they will not appear before Christ on the Day of Judgment.
- Jesus has been appointed by God to judge this world.
- We all will appear before the *Judgment Seat of Christ* and give account of ourselves.
- We all will be judged by the *works* we've done in the flesh.
- Although it is true that we are free from the law and are now under grace, this doesn't mean we allow our faith to stagnate and die. Faith without works is dead and belief alone is not enough. Satan himself believes in God.
- Faith and works compliment each other and both are integral parts of being Christian.
- Jesus and the Apostles indicated that we must still obey the Commandments.
- Christians are known for their good works and are eager to do them.
- We must be doers, not just hearers.
- Some Christians have been led into thinking that they can go on sinning once they've been "saved" without adversely affecting their chances of entering the Kingdom of God. But the Bible says Christians must do their best to keep from sinning.
- Belief in Christ is not assurance into Heaven. There will be some believers who will not enter the Kingdom of God. Many examples cited.
- When Christ came, the emphasis on faith and works was reversed.
- Abraham's obedience was just as important as his faith.

15

- The original Greek & Hebrew words for faith and trust are never used interchangeably in the Bible. They're two different things. Trusting is faith in action.
- Every Christian is given a certain amount of talents and he is expected to use them fully and wisely. It is our duty to do them; that's why we were given them.
- Judgment is both a necessity and a certainty.

CHAPTER TWO: THE PRETRIBULATION RAPTURE

- Definition of the term "tribulation".
- Brief explanation of "the great tribulation" & "seven-year tribulation theories".
- The tribulation period may or may not last for exactly seven years. This notion is merely guesswork.
- Definition of the term "rapture".
- Brief explanation for the term "millennium" and its place in prophecy.
- Pre/ Mid/ Posttribulation rapture theories explained.

CHAPTER THREE: CHRISTIANS IN TRIBULATION

- Tribulation separates true Christians from false Christians.
- We are exposed to trials and tribulations to teach us patience, forbearance, obedience, and how to trust in God.
- The methods utilized by God to correct the Children of Israel are not efficacious for correcting Christians because Christians are not centralized into an isolated area as the Children of Israel were.
- Physical sins of Israel and spiritual sins of Christians.
- Physical tribulation is designed to correct the spiritual person.
- Old Testament passages quoted showing that God always has tested His chosen ones.
- New Testament passages quoted showing that God always has, does now, and always will test and prove His elect.

- Even Jesus was tested like us in all ways.
- It was necessary for Christ to experience physical trials and temptations so He could assist us in our varied trials.
- Tribulation can only strengthen a true believer; but a false Christian is ground to powder thereby.
- Our *"reward"* is in Heaven. Rewards are never given for nothing; they are given to someone for doing that which is difficult. But what sort of reward should we expect if we attempt to evade our trial?
- If Christ, His Disciples, John the Baptist, all the Old Testament prophets, and all the good Christians of the past weren't exempt from tribulation, then why should Christians of today expect to be treated any differently?

CHAPTER FOUR: FALSE DOCTRINE AND THE WRATH OF GOD

- Christians are not *"appointed to wrath"*. But there's a big difference between God's wrath and tribulation.
- The wrath of God is not only reserved for the wicked; it is also reserved for Christians who follow false doctrine.
- When we stray from the truth, we are in danger of believing a lie.
- The pretribulation theory = A pleasant-sounding doctrine.
- We shouldn't believe what we hear about the Bible just because some well-known person told us or because it sounds logical.
- Theories are theories. They are not fact. When a theory is introduced as irrefutable truth, does it not become a lie?
- Great faith vs. little doubt.
- We shouldn't be mingling theories with our faith.
- If we interfuse conjecture with belief, our own proud interpretations could cause unnecessary divisions within the Church.
- Our proud interpretations are beginning to reduce the most blessed sacraments of Christianity into the same kinds of meaningless rituals that circumcision ultimately became to the Children of Israel.
- The only important things: God, Christ, and the Holy Spirit

- We need to follow the example of Christ.
- Every single conception of the Bible must be scrupulously examined before including it in our "Creed of Faith"
- If you ask the Lord for wisdom and guidance He will give them to you freely and abundantly.

CHAPTER FIVE: THE GOSPELS VS THE RAPTURE

- "Author's Hypothetical Tribulation Outline". Possible events to transpire during the tribulation period.
- What might happen to the faith of those who trust in this rapture if it fails to transpire before these trying times?
- Matt. 24, Mark 13, & Luke 21 do not pertain only to the time of their composition.
- Matt. 24, Mark 13, & Luke 21 are not predictions of gathering Jews to Palestine.
- There's no difference between Jews and Christians; both are the children of God. The term *"elect"* designates all believers in general.
- Matt. 24, Mark 13, & Luke 21 as "dual prophecies". This may be so but regardlessly, they definitely do concern the Second Advent of our Lord Jesus Christ.
- Begin explaining Matthew 24 verse by verse.
- Christ's account of the tribulation period preceding His Coming is one uninterrupted sequence of events. He leaves no room for the pretribulational rapture.
- Matt. 24:4-7 given at length and explained. Wars, famines, droughts, false christs, earthquakes, etc. will take place during the tribulation period.
- The end of the world vs. the end of an age.
- Matt. 24:9-10 provided.
- Matt. 24:11-13 provided and explained. Only the Christians who endure this period of time *"unto the end shall be saved."*
- Daniel's *"abomination of desolation."*

18

- This period of adversity could be especially severe within a major city.
- Matt. 24:19-21 provided. This time of trouble will be very hard on women who are either expecting or nursing children.
- I realize these tribulations sound intimidating. I'm not attempting to frighten you; I'm trying to warn you.
- Should we fear death and adversity, or should we fear God?
- To fear death is a direct contradiction to our faith in Christ's resurrection.
- God certainly knows how to reserve His elect from excessive suffering. But that doesn't mean He will translate them into the Kingdom of God.
- Enoch & Elijah were exceptions to the rule, not standards. These were extraordinary people & extraordinary events.
- There's no difference between this rapture and death.
- A Christian's physical death is actually his spiritual birth.
- The Disciples longed to die so they could be with our Lord.
- If there were no fear of death and/or tribulation within the Christian community, what need or even desire would there be for a pretribulation rapture?
- Christ will *"shorten the days"* of this period of distress for His elect's sake.
- False christs will possess the unusual ability to perform *"great signs and wonders"* in the sight of men. These impostors will perform **genuine miracles**. The original Greek words for *"signs"* and *"wonders"* are *"semeion"* and *"teras"* respectively. These are the same words used in the Bible to describe the fantastic miracles performed by Christ and His Disciples.
- Some possible miracles of false christs portrayed.
- What might happen to the Christian who walks up to this intruder and denounces him in the presence of everyone?
- Christians will be executed by their own friends and relatives during this time.
- Jesus certainly wouldn't have warned us of all these things if we

weren't going to be here when they came to pass.
- The pretribulation rapture = A second chance at entering Heaven.
- The pretribulation rapture vs the last judgment.
- When Christ really comes every single person on earth will know precisely what is happening.
- Jesus returns **after** the tribulation period.
- Begin methodically explaining Mark 13:5-27 verse by verse.
- Mark 13:5-10 provided at length. This reading warns of the same kinds of things as the Gospel of St. Matthew.
- Christians will be strengthened and guided by the Holy Spirit during this time.
- Martyrdom, the great privilege.
- Presumptuousness, a precarious position.
- Again, Jesus comes **after** the tribulation period.
- These prophecies lead up to the *"end."* When we examine this Greek word and its original meaning, we find that it is clear that Christ meant the Church would remain here on earth right up to the end of time.
- Luke 21:8-28 provided at length.
- Again, Jesus comes **after** the tribulation period.
- Luke 21:36: The word *"escape"* does not implicate a rapture.
- Begin explaining Luke 17:20-37 verse by verse.
- Luke 17 refers to the same chain of events as Matt. 24, Mark 13, and Luke 21, only in slightly different words.
- Luke 17:26-37 = These verses are often taken out of context by rapture teachers. But these passages allude to Christ's Second Coming and the judgment; not the rapture.
- Tribulation period summarized in 10 events.

CHAPTER SIX: THE EPISTLES VS THE RAPTURE

- Six passages often quoted by rapture advocates delineated.
- I Thess. 4:13-14 provided and simplified.

- I Thess. 4:15 indicates Jesus' Second Advent.
- I Thess. 4:16, Jesus Returns *with "the voice of the archangel"* and *"with the trump(et) of God."* These things indicate our Lord's Second Coming, the resurrection, and the end of the world, not a pretribulation rapture.
- The resurrection transpires on *"the last day."*
- Those who believe in both the rapture and the millennium are actually saying there are three resurrections.
- I Thess. 4:17-18, Jesus comes *"in the clouds."* This is another clear indication that Paul is speaking of Christ's Second Advent here.
- Jesus' Second Coming vs invisible rapture.
- The pretribulation rapture = three comings of Christ.
- I Thess. 4:13-18 simplified.
- The truth is plain and simple; it shouldn't be changed.
- A person does not need another human being to teach him about God. Christ will teach him.
- II Thessalonians & Jude 14 explained. There's no difference between Jesus coming to be glorified *"with"* His saints or *"in"* His saints. The original Greek words in these two passages are identical and mean exactly the same thing.
- II Thess. 2:1 does not implicate a pretribulation rapture. Both of these events take place on the same *"day."*
- 34 references provided regarding *"the day of Christ."*
- II Thess 2:3-4 provided. Satan is working his way into the pulpit.
- Satan has the power to appear righteous.
- II Thess. 2:5-7 provided at length and explained.
- It is not the Church that is hampering this *"son of perdition"* from being revealed. The Church is never mentioned in the Bible in the masculine gender.
- II Thess. 2:8-12 provided and explained. Christians who stray from the truth are in danger of following the false doctrine of this son of perdition.
- I Corinthians 15:50-53 given at length and clarified. This passage doesn't even mention the tribulation period. How then can a

pretribulation theory even be constructed from this?
- I Corinthians 15:50-53 simplified.
- Titus 2:13-14 provided and explained.
- This passage should be used to contradict the pretribulation rapture concept, not as evidence supporting it. The Greek word for *"appearing"* in this reading indicates a visible event, not an invisible rapture.

CHAPTER SEVEN: CLOSING NOTES ON THE RAPTURE THEORY

- Rapture advocates are really saying to the Christian community, "Peace, peace!" When there is no peace.
- Rapture proponents have built a protective wall around Christians that doesn't belong there.
- Statement given by evangelist Jimmy Swaggart conceding an element of risk associated with the rapture theory.
- Logical arguments cannot be fabricated against truth.
- If there is **any chance whatsoever** of this rapture failing to transpire before these trying times, it is not worthy of wholehearted belief. It's that simple.
- Anyone who disagrees with this concept and allows it to continue unchallenged is adding onto the problem.
- Being skeptical about this (or any other) man-made concept absolutely will not jeopardize your chances of participating in it. God expects this.
- If this idea contains a trace of risk or uncertainty it should not be included in our faith.
- Closing exhortation for this chapter.

CHAPTER EIGHT: THE MILLENNIUM

- The millennium: Revelation 20:1-15 provided in its entirety.
- The millennial theory is much older than the rapture Theory and

is far more embedded into Christian thought.
• Brief outline of upcoming chapters dealing with the millennium in order to give my readers an idea of how I intend to address this concept.

CHAPTER NINE: JESUS' SECOND ADVENT VS THE MILLENNIUM

• Christ will judge between the righteous & the wicked at His coming. He is not going to "put judgment off" for a thousand years.
• Christ's Second Coming/ the rapture or assumption of the elect/ the resurrection/ the last judgment/ and the end of the world are all one and the same event. There's not a thousand-year period between any two of those events.
• Christ's Second Coming summarized in thirteen events.

CHAPTER TEN: THE MILLENNIUM & FALSE CHRISTS

• The millennial concept sets the perfect stage for the appearance of false christs.
• We are told by Jesus to disbelieve anyone who claims to be Christ no matter what he might say or do.
• When our Lord really comes every single person upon the face of the earth will know He is authentic, dead or alive.
• The immense power of false christs.
• When Jesus first came His miracles were proof of His authenticity. But when false christs arrive, their miracles will be proof of their fraudulence.
• Three fundamental methods for "testing" a prophet discussed and why they would be useless in determining a false christ.
• The miracles of false christs would have a much greater impact when there is a need for them.
• False christs vs the antichrist.
• We must live by faith and not by sight.

CHAPTER ELEVEN: TAMPERING WITH THE REVELATION

- Nobody completely understands the Apocalypse. Theories have no place with whole-hearted belief. It is dangerous to introduce conjecture as irrefutable truth. Any theory constructed from symbolical prophecy is quite worthy of skepticism and quite unworthy of unwavering faith. To claim to completely understand the meanings of the complex symbols of the apocalypse is to claim to be a prophet. The Revelation means many different things to many different people. If any of these theories divide the Church or contains an element of risk, they are worthy only of the trash bin.
- Alternative mode of interpretation for the millennium provided.

CHAPTER TWELVE: THE EVERLASTING KINGDOMS

- Any kingdom of the Old Testament which is said to last indefinitely is not a prediction about the millennium because the millennium does not last forever.
- 39 everlasting kingdoms of the Old Testament delineated.
- This earth is transitory; it will not endure forever either. Hence these everlasting kingdoms cannot possibly occur upon this earth.
- Perhaps these kingdoms will be instituted on the "new earth" or in the "new heaven?" I don't know for certain but we do know these kingdoms last forever and our Lord will dwell among His people in them.
- Christ's kingdom is spiritual in nature and its foundations are set in our hearts. Christ's kingdom lasts forever but the millennium doesn't.

CHAPTER THIRTEEN: THE BATTLE WITH GOG AND MAGOG

- The word "*saints*" was a common expression in the Bible. This designates all believers in general.

- If it is at all possible that Revelation's Gog and Ezekiel's Gog are identical twins, then the theories of many chiliasts will be found to be in serious error.
- Many chiliasts claim that Ezekiel's Gog is Russia and its massive military thrust into the oil-rich countries of the Middle East. But they claim Revelation's Gog represents something entirely different.
- Eight major similarities between Revelation's Gog and Ezekiel's Gog illustrated.
- The Targum of Jonathan ben Uzziel & the Jerusalem Targum.
- To agree that these two entities might be the same means we need to treat them as though they were. If the possibility cannot be ruled out, it would be irresponsible to treat them as though they were positively different entities.

CHAPTER FOURTEEN: CLOSING NOTES ON THE MILLENNIUM

- A review of all the major points about the millennium provided.
- The millennial concept could become a "stumbling block" to the Christian community.

25

CHAPTER ONE

ANTINOMIANISM IN THE CHURCH

There are a couple of common misconceptions among the Christian community that I feel need to be addressed and clarified at this point. Many Christians have come to believe that abstinence from sin and doing good works are "unimportant" because God already knows who is His and who isn't (II Tim. 2:19), and Christians are saved by faith and grace, not works. This has led to varying degrees of antinomianism in the Church, (Gr. *anti*, "against"; *nomos*, "law"). This belief teaches that since Christians have been freed from the Mosaic Law, they can go on sinning and that good works are "unnecessary" because they've already been predestined for salvation, (Rom. 8:28-33; Eph. 1:4, 11-12), and God foreknows who is going to Heaven, (I Pet. 1:2). But these people need to remind themselves that although this is true, there are others who are predestined to destruction as well, (Rom. 9:16-23; I Pet. 2:8; Jude 4). We need to be careful not to fall into the latter category by assuming we're already in the former, (cf. Matt. 20:16; Luke 18:9-14; Rom. 11:20-22; 12:3; I Cor. 10:10-12; Gal. 6:3). This was already becoming a problem in Paul's time, (Rom. 3:8; Jude 4). Christians were abusing their freedom from the Law to continue in their sins, (Rom. 6:1-6, 15; 7:1-12).

Predestination is a Biblical paradox and the key to its secret lies outside the parameters of time, (Matt. 25:34; Luke 11:50; John 17:24; Acts 2:23; Rom. 16:25; Col. 1:26-27; II Thess. 2:13; II Tim. 1:9; Heb. 4:3; I Pet. 1:20). Man's mind is earthly and a slave to time. It is incapable of venturing outside these boundaries. But God is unaffected by time. The history of mankind is but an infinitely decreasing moment in an infinitely increasing sea of timelessness until it eventually becomes a kind of "Schwarzschild radius of time" to the Lord. I am convinced that predestination, like symbolical prophecy, cannot be fully understood without direct divine assistance. (See my observations about time, space, and the value of pi on pages 149-150.) Many Christians and philosophers have made dangerous and foolish statements about it, including yours truly. Every person who has made an attempt to explain predestination has failed miserably. I could "poke holes" in every single theory I've read. And until someone explains it accurately and completely I certainly wouldn't stake my soul on it. We all would do better to think of predestination as an effect of God's foreknowlege at the point of creation, not its cause. This does no injustice to God's omniscience, scripture, or the free will of man. St. Augustine summed up the matter rather well when he said: "We should act as though everything depended upon us, and pray as though everything depended upon God."

Antinomianism has always been a big concern of mine. But I thought that I could avoid the issue in this work because it seemed to be unrelated to the pretribulation rapture concept. But the more I thought about it the more I realized that this belief may be the very reason for this concept's birth and popularity. This belief is the reason why Christians have been convinced that they need not experience tribulation or even appear before Christ on the Day of Judgment. Since these individuals presume they are already going to heaven and Christians *"are not appointed to wrath"* (Rom. 5:9-10; I Thess. 1:9-10; 5:9-10), they see no need for these things. This belief also teaches that Christians are not responsible for doing good works because salvation is attained by faith and grace alone and they, therefore, will not be held accountable for their actions no matter what they do. But this viewpoint is misleading and creates a false sense of security. It could also lead to laziness, spiritual complacency, presumptuousness, and self-righteousness.

Jesus has been appointed by God to judge this world, (Matt. 3:11-

12; Luke 3:17; John 5:22, 27; Acts 10:42; 17:31; Rom. 2:4-9,16; James 5:7-9). *__Judgment begins at the House of God__*, (I Pet. 4:5, 17-19). We all will appear before the *"Judgment Seat of Christ"* and give account of ourselves, (Matt. 12:36; Gal. 6:5). Paul wrote:

"For to this end Christ both died, and rose, and revived, that he might be Lord both of the dead and the living. But why dost thou judge thy brother? Or why dost thou set at nought thy brother? __For we shall all stand before the judgment seat of Christ__. For it is written, As I live, saith the Lord, every knee shall bow to me, and every tongue shall confess to God. __So then every one of us shall give account of himself to God__." (Rom. 14:9-12)

St. Paul again:

"__For we must all appear before the judgment seat of Christ__; that every one may receive the things done in his body, according to that he hath done, __whether it be good or bad__. (II Cor. 5:10)

We all will be judged by the *__works__* we've done in the flesh, (Rom. 2:6; I Cor. 3:8; II Cor. 11:15; II Tim. 4:14; I Pet. 1:17; Rev. 2:23; 20:12-13; 22:12). Even Jesus said:

"For the Son of man shall come in the glory of his Father with His angels; and then he shall __reward every man according to his works__." (Matt. 16:27)

Whether or not we are accounted worthy of the Kingdom of Heaven does not depend solely upon our faith but also upon our actions here on earth. Christians who have done good will go to Heaven while those who have done evil descend into Hell. Jesus again:

"Marvel not at this: for the hour is coming, in the which all that are in the graves shall hear his voice, And shall come forth; __they that have done good, unto the resurrection of life; and they that have done evil, unto the resurrection of damnation__." (John 5:28-29)

Yes, it is true that our faith in Christ leads to salvation (Luke 12:8-9; John 11:25-27; Acts 16:31; Rom. 10:9-13) and keeps us from condemnation (John 3:16-18; 5:24; Rom. 8:1; I Cor. 1:8). And we are no longer under the Law because Christ came to free us from the

Law, (Gal. 3:1-10). If justification came by the Law then Christ died for nothing: (Gal. 2:21). If we seek to be justified by the Law, then we have fallen from grace: (Gal. 5:4). Grace is the gift of God; it cannot be earned through works, (Eph. 2:8-9), not even martyrdom, (I Cor. 13:3). Hence, we are justified by faith and grace, not works, (Rom. 3:20-31; 9:11, 32; 11:6; Gal. 2:15-21; Phil. 3:9; II Tim. 1:9; Titus 3:5).

But just because we are under grace doesn't mean that we allow our faith to stagnate and die. Belief in God and Christ is not enough to enter heaven. If that were the only criteria for entrance into the Kingdom of God, Satan himself would be there also. Faith without works is dead and belief alone is not enough. As it is written:

"What doth it profit, my brethren, though a man say he have faith, and have not works? Can faith save him? If a brother or sister be naked, and destitute of daily food, And one of you say unto them, Depart in peace, be ye warmed and filled; notwithstanding ye give them not those things which are needful to the body; what doth it profit? Even so faith, if it hath not works, is dead, being alone. Yea, a man may say, Thou hast faith, and I have works: show me thy faith without thy works, and I will show thee my faith by my works. Thou believest that there is one God; thou doest well: the devils also believe, and tremble. But wilt thou know, O vain man, that faith without works is dead? Was not Abraham our father justified by works, when he had offered Isaac his son upon the alter? Seest thou how faith wrought with his works, and by works was faith made perfect? And the Scripture was fulfilled which saith, Abraham believed God, and it was imputed unto him for righteousness: and he was called the friend of God. Ye see then how that by works a man is justified, and not by faith only. Likewise also was not Rahab the harlot justified by works, when she had received the messengers, and had sent them out another way? For as the body without the spirit is dead, so faith without works is dead also." (James 2:14-26).

I've heard some people attempt to "explain away" this passage. It's a fascinating thing to watch. Some have even ventured to say utterly preposterous and outrageous things about it because it doesn't fit into their conception of salvation. Martin Luther said this epistle "is an epistle of straw, fit only to be burnt". Should we also burn the Gospels then, since Christ Himself says essentially the same thing about doing good deeds?

*"When the Son of man shall come in his glory, and all the holy angels with him, then shall he sit upon the throne of his glory: And before him shall be gathered all nations: and he shall separate them one from another, as a shepherd divideth his sheep from his goats: And he shall set the sheep on his right hand, but the goats on the left. Then shall the King say unto them on his right hand, Come, ye blessed of my Father, inherit the kingdom prepared for you from the foundation of the world: For I was ahungered, **and ye gave me meat** (James 2:16): I was thirsty, **and ye gave me** drink: I was a stranger, **and ye took me in**: Naked, **and ye clothed me**: I was sick, **and ye visited me**: I was in prison, **and ye came unto me**. Then shall the righteous answer him, saying, Lord, when saw we thee ahungered, and fed thee? Or thirsty, and gave thee drink? When saw we thee a stranger, and took thee in? Or naked, and clothed thee? Or when saw we thee sick, or in prison, and came unto thee? And the King shall answer and say unto them, Verily I say unto you, **Inasmuch as ye have done it unto one of the least of these my brethren, ye have done it unto me**. Then shall he say also unto them on the left hand, Depart from me, ye cursed, into everlasting fire, prepared for the devil and his angels: For I was ahungered, **and ye gave me no meat**: I was thirsty, **and ye gave me no drink**: I was a stranger, **and ye took me not in**: Naked, **and ye clothed me not**: Sick, and in prison, **and ye visited me not**. Then shall they also answer him, saying, Lord, when saw we thee ahungered, or athirst, or a stranger, or naked, or sick, or in prison, **and did not minister unto thee**? Then shall he answer them, saying, Verily I say unto you, **Inasmuch as ye did it not to one of the least of these, ye did it not to me**. And these shall go away into everlasting punishment: but the righteous into life eternal."* (Matt. 25:31-46)

Doing good works is definitely a major theme of the Bible taught both by Christ and His Disciples. There are at least as many passages dealing with our responsibility to do good works as there are dealing with justification by faith and grace. Now I'm not trying to diminish the merits of faith and grace, but establish them. Faith and grace absolutely supersede good works. Faith without works is dead. But works without faith is worse. Doing good works is the Christian's way of showing his love for his neighbor. A Christian can have all the faith in the world and it will be utterly worthless without love, (I Cor. 13:2). Faith is to works what primer is to paint. The first necessarily precedes the second and the second necessarily follows the first. As St. James explains, neither is sufficient alone; but they depend upon each other to complete the task. Just as primer alone does not provide adequate protection until the paint is applied. Even so, faith alone is not sufficient without works being applied. Hence, faith and works compliment each other and both are integral parts of being Christian. And even though we are not under the Law, it is still holy, (Rom. 7:12). Jesus said we must still obey the Ten Commandments, (Matt. 5:17-20; 19:16-19; Mark 10:18-22; Luke 18:18-20; John 15:10). If we are God's children we need to show it by doing His Commandments, (I Cor. 7:19; I John 3:22-24; 5:2-3; II John 4-6). If we obey God's Holy Commandments we will have a clear conscience, (Acts 23:1; I Tim. 1:5; Heb. 9:14) and our hearts won't condemn us, (I John 3:21-24). If we say we know God but continue to disobey the Commandments, we are liars, (Titus 1:16; I John 2:1-12).

The Lord will try every man's work to see if it withstands the test. If our work survives the test we will be rewarded, (Rom. 2:10; Eph. 6:8). But if it doesn't we will suffer loss, (I Cor. 3:13-15) Although we are not saved by doing good deeds, we are still expected to do them, (Eph. 2:8-10). Christians should try to inspire and encourage one another to do good deeds, (Heb. 10:24; James 3:13; Titus 3:8). A true Christian is recognized by his good works, (Matt. 5:16; 7:20; Mark 14:6-9; Luke 10:42; John 3:19-21; Acts 9:36; 26:20; Rom. 13:3; 15:2,18; I Cor. 15:58; 16:10; II Cor. 9:8; 10:11; Gal. 6:4, 10; Col. 1:10; 3:17; I Thess. 5:13; II Thess. 2:17; I Tim. 2:10; 5:10,

25; 6:17-19; II Tim. 2:15, 21; 3:17; 4:5; Titus 2:7; 3:1, 14; Heb. 6:10; 13:21; I Pet. 2:12; Rev. 2:2, 5, 9, 13, 19, 23, 26; 3:1, 2, 8, 15). A true Christian is eager to do good works, (Gal. 4:18; Titus 2:14). Christians are to perform their good deeds anonymously when possible so as not to draw attention to themselves or receive praise from others, (Matt. 6:1-4; 23:3-5). A true Christian acts out of the goodness in his heart, (Matt. 12:35) and expects nothing in return from others for his charitable works, (Luke 6:33-35). A Christian without works is like salt without flavor, (Mark 9:50; Luke 14:34). The person who does good things is of God, (III John 11), but he that does evil deeds is of Satan, (Luke 11:47-51; John 8:41-47; II Cor. 11:13; Phil. 3:2-3; III John 10-11; Jude15). Even the mighty works of Christ bore witness that He was from God, (Matt. 11:20, 21, 23; 13:54; Mark 6:2; Luke 10:13-15; 19:37-38; John 10:25, 32, 33, 37, 38; 15:24; Acts 10:38). We are all fellow workers in Christ, (Rom. 16:21; I Cor. 3:8-9; 12:29-30; 15:58; II Cor. 6:1; Phil. 4:3; I Thess. 3:2), and are worthy of our wages, (Matt. 10:10; Luke 10:7; I Tim. 5:18), which is to be written in the Book of Life, (Phil. 4:3). But what wages should we hope to receive if we don't do any work?

The Bible says faith alone is inadequate; we must be doers not just hearers, (Mark 3:35; Luke 8:21; Rom. 2:12-16; I John 3:16-18). As St. James explains:

*" Wherefore lay apart all filthiness and superfluity of naughtiness, and receive with meekness the engrafted word, which is able to save your souls. **But be ye doers of the word, and not hearers only, deceiving your own selves**. For if any be a hearer of the word, and not a doer, he is like unto a man beholding his natural face in a glass: For he beholdeth himself, and goeth his way, and straightway forgetteth what manner of man he was. But whoso looketh into the perfect law of liberty, and continueth therein, **he being not a forgetful hearer, but a doer of the work, this man shall be blessed in his deed**. If any man among you seem to be religious, and bridleth not his tongue, but deceiveth his own heart, this man's religion is vain. Pure religion and undefiled before God and the Father is this, **To visit the fatherless and widows in their affliction**, and to keep himself*

unspotted from the world." (James 1:21-27).

Jesus Christ said the same thing:

*"And why call ye me, Lord, Lord, and do not the things which I say? Whosoever cometh to me, **and heareth my sayings, and doeth them**, I will show you to whom he is like: He is like a man which built a house, and digged deep, and laid the foundation on a rock: and when the flood arose, the stream beat vehemently upon that house, **and could not shake it: for it was founded upon a rock**. **But he that heareth, and doeth not**, is like a man that without a foundation built a house upon the earth; against which the stream did beat vehemently, **and immediately it fell; and the ruin of that house was great**." (Luke 6:46-49).*

I've often heard people say that they no longer have to worry about Judgment Day because they are going to Heaven whether they sin or not. Make no mistake about it, Satan is a serious threat to all Christians, (Matt. 16:23; Mark 4:15; 8:33; Luke 8:12; 22:31; John 13:2; Acts 5:3; 26:18; I Cor. 7:5; 10:20-21; II Cor. 2:10-11; 11:14; 12:7; Eph. 4:27; 6:10-12; I Thess. 2:18; 3:5; II Thess. 2:9; I Tim. 3:6-7; 4:1; 5:14-15; II Tim. 2:26; James 4:7; I Pet. 5:8-9; Rev. 9:20; 12:9) and is determined to destroy us. There's nothing he would like more than to have us believe we are already going to Heaven no matter what we do. This is the ultimate lie, (Rom. 3:8; 6:1-6; Jude 4). While it is true that none of us is perfect, (Rom. 3:23; Gal. 3:22; I John 1:5-10), this is no excuse for not trying to be, (Matt. 5:48; Rom. 7:13-25; II Cor. 7:1; Eph. 4:13; 5:1; Phil. 3:15; Col. 4:12; II Tim. 3:17; James 1:4; 3:2). Christ came so sinners may obtain redemption of sins, (Eph. 1:7-14; Col. 1:14) and we should live like free men; but we shouldn't use that as a pretext to sin, (Gal. 5:13-25; I Pet. 2:16). And we shouldn't abuse grace by deliberately committing sins, (Rom. 6:1-13). If we reject our conscience we make shipwreck of our faith, (I Tim. 1:19-20). If we yield to sin while under grace we are the servant of sin, (John 8:34) and this leads to death, (Rom. 6:16; 8:13). Sinning deliberately after receiving the Holy Spirit leads to condemnation, (Heb. 10:26-31). We should put away sinful lusts, (Mark 4:19; Rom. 6:12; 13:14; Eph. 2:3; II Tim. 2:22; Titus 2:12;

3:3; James 1:14-15; I Pet. 1:14; 2:11; 4:2-3; II Pet. 2:10, 18; Jude 16, 18) and not grieve the Spirit, (Eph. 4:22-32). A true Christian refrains from sin, (Acts 10:35; Rom. 12:9, 21; 16:19; I Cor. 6:12-20; 8:12; 10:10-12; 15:34; Gal. 6:7-10; Eph. 5:3-5; Col. 1:21-23; 3:24-25; I Thess. 5:15; Heb. 3:11-19; 4:1-3, 11; James 4:8; I Pet. 3:10-12; I John 2:1; 5:18-20; II John 8-9). Christians who commit sin risk falling from grace, (Heb. 12:12-16). If God didn't spare the angels when they fell, He's not going to spare us either, (II Pet. 2:4). We are supposed to abstain from sin, follow after righteousness, and fight the good fight of faith, (I Cor. 9:25-27; I Tim. 1:18; 6:11-12; II Tim. 4:7). If we continue to sin God does not abide in us because His nature wouldn't allow it; you can tell the children of God from the children of Satan by their actions, (I John 3:4-10). We shouldn't keep company with people who deliberately sin, (I Cor. 5:9-13; 15:33; II Cor. 6:14-15; II Thess. 3:6-7) because we might lose our own stability, (II Pet. 3:17-18). We need to work out our own salvation, (Phil. 2:12), and press ever forward toward the mark, (II Tim. 4:7; Heb. 4:11-13), but not as though we have already attained it, (Rom. 8:24-25; Phil. 3:12-15). When we see our brother sin, it is our responsibility to point it out and restore him gently, (II Cor. 2:5-8; Gal. 6:1-5; II Thess. 3:14-15; I Tim. 5:1-2). If we turn him to God he will be saved, (II Tim. 2:25-26) and a multitude of sins will be hidden, (James 5:19-20). If we do sin we need to repent, (Acts 3:19) and this will lead to forgiveness, (Eph. 1:7; Col. 1:14; I John 2:12), Godly grief (II Cor 7:9-11), and salvation, (Heb. 12:1-11). Because there is great joy in Heaven over one penitent sinner, (Luke 15:10, 18-24).

As I indicated earlier, belief in Christ alone is not enough to enter the Kingdom of Heaven. Jesus said many believers will say to Him in the Day of Judgment, *"Lord Lord,"* but He will say, *"I never knew you"* (Matt. 7:21-23; Luke 13:24-30). Many Christians accept the Lord. But after being cleansed from their sins they return again to their old ways and are seven times worse than they were to begin with, (Matt. 12:43-45; II Pet. 2:18-22). Christians can shrink when tribulation arrives, (Matt. 13:20-22; Mark 4:14-17; Luke 8:11-13; Heb. 10:36-39). Christians can jeopardize their salvation through love of money, (Matt. 19:21-24; Mark 4:18-19; 10:21-23; Luke 12:14-15; I Tim. 6:9-10). Christians who are self-righteous and think they are better than others are guilty of sin, (II Cor. 10:18; Phil. 2:3; James 2:9), but penitent sinners will be justified, (Luke 18:13-14). If Christians don't care for their family they will lose their reward, (I Tim. 5:7-8). Christians who preach or follow false doctrine will be led to wrath and condemnation, (Rom. 1:17-25; 2:5-9; Gal. 1:6-9; Eph. 5:6-7; Col. 2:4, 8; II Thess. 2:10-12; I Tim. 6:20-21). Christians who defile their bodies, the Temple of the Lord, (II Cor. 6:16-18) will be destroyed by God, (I Cor. 3:16-17). Christians who taste of the Holy Spirit and then reject it, crucify Christ afresh and are condemned, (Heb. 6:4-8). A Christian who is doing good for his fellow man when Christ comes will be greatly rewarded. But if that Christian begins to eat and drink with the drunken and beat his fellow servants, the Lord will cut this person out of the land of living and appoint him his portion with the hypocrites, (Matt. 24:45-51; Luke 12:42-46). If a Christian's hand causes him to sin, he should cut it off. It is better to enter Heaven maimed than to descend into Hell with your whole body, (Mark 9:43-48). God has given each Christian a certain amount of talents and we are expected to use them, (Rom. 12:4-8; I Cor. 12:1-11; 14:1-39; Eph. 4:4-8). If we don't, we shall be thrown into outer darkness, (Matt. 25:14-30, 31-46; Luke 19:11-27). We're not to hide our light under a bushel. We are expected to let it shine for all to see our good works, (Matt. 5:14-16; Luke 11:33-36), so don't accept the grace of God in vain, (I Cor. 15:2; II Cor. 6:1; Gal. 3:4). Every true Christian is expected to bring forth good fruit, (Matt. 7:11-19; 13:37-39; Luke 6:43-45; 8:15). But if he is unproductive, he will be cast into the fire, (Matt. 3:10; 13:4-42, 47-50; Luke 3:9; John 15:1-6). Christians have to give their best effort. The widow who put in two mites will be justified before believers who gave more, but only out of convenience, (Mark 12:41-44; Luke 21:1-4). Christians who put their hand to the plow and look back will not be accounted worthy of the Kingdom of Heaven, (Luke 9:62). The Jews are the original branches of our Lord's proverbial tree. Those branches were broken off so that the Gentiles might be grafted on. If the wild branches (Gentiles) boast against the original branches (Jews), God will cut us off and graft on again the original branches, (Rom. 11:17-24). A Christian who knows the Will of God and fails to do it is committing sin, (James 4:17). It would be better for him not to know it to begin with than to fail to do it after knowing it, (II Pet. 2:21-22). And there are many more passages dealing with this topic.

There's no doubt about it that faith and good works go hand in hand. Good works follow faith around like a lost puppy. Where faith is found, good works are never far behind. And if good works are not to be found, then neither is faith. In the Old Testament, emphasis was placed on doing acts based upon the Mosaic Law. These acts were very elaborate and had to be followed to the letter to attain absolution and justification. But this was found to be ineffective for two fundamental reasons: First of all, the Mosaic Law couldn't produce faith, (Gal. 3:11-12), and this was becoming routine and ritualistic. The Children of Israel were beginning to abuse the Law by thinking that they could go on sinning as long as they came to the altar and performed their elaborate sacrifices. The second is because the blood of animals could not bring about a clear conscience and could not reconcile us fully to God, (Heb. 9:9-14; 10:1-18). A new and better sacrifice was needed, the Body and Blood of our Lord Jesus Christ. When Jesus came, the emphasis on faith and works was reversed, (Gal. 3:23-29). Justification now is attained by faith and not by acts of the Law. In the Old Testament the emphasis centered upon works; and works without faith was dead, (Rom. 9:30-32). In the New Testament the emphasis centers on faith; and faith without works is just as dead, (James 2:14-26).

Suppose Abraham, knowing the infinite mercy and grace of God, said within himself, "The Lord is very gracious and of tender mercy. I therefore will not go to the place He wants me to go nor do the things which He commands me to do, for it will only be a waste of time and effort because I have faith that He will spare my son." Would Abraham have been justified in this? Of course not, this would be nothing short of disobedience. Abraham's obedience during this event was just as important as his faith, (Gen. 22:16-18). Abraham had to prepare for his journey, take up his only son Isaac, wander for three days in the desert, climb to the top of Mount Moriah, construct an altar of stone, lay his son thereon, and draw the knife to slay him before the Angel of the Lord stopped him. This was not only difficult for Abraham spiritually and emotionally. But it was also hard on him physically. Abraham was over a hundred years old at the time. He died of old age shortly thereafter. So it was not faith alone that justified Abraham, but the **act of faith**. Since the Lord foreknows all things He obviously knew beforehand what the outcome of the entire event would be. And since Abraham already had faith that God would keep all His promises and that He would spare his son, then why did the Lord bother to command him to do all these things? This was to show Abraham how to fully appreciate God's mercy and that **trusting** in the Lord is the only means of salvation.

The original Hebrew and Greek words for faith and trust are never used interchangeably in the Bible; they are two different things. Faith is easy to acquire and a secure place to be. Faith is always a noun in the Bible; it can be possessed. Trust is almost always used as a verb in the Bible; it is something a person does. Trust is faith in faith, hope in hope, faith in action, faith complete (Rom. 4:17-25), and can only be attained when faith is tried. A person can have faith without trusting in God but cannot trust in God without having faith. It is easy to have faith that God will rescue you from a dangerous thing. But you don't know what it is to trust until you are actually faced with it. The difference between faith and trusting is a lot like the difference between belief and knowing. A person can believe a thing and not know it but he cannot know a thing and not believe it. Only when his belief is subjected to a probative test can he know whether he is right or wrong. When a person faces adversity and trusts in God his faith is being confirmed in a similar way. When God delivers him from this difficulty he knows that his faith is credible and is assured that it has not been misplaced. The more times this occurs and the same results achieved, the more faith increases and strengthens while doubt decreases and weakens. If this be continued, doubt is eventually eliminated altogether and the following Words of Christ become reality:

" *Verily I say unto you,* ___If ye have faith, and doubt not___*, ye shall not only do this which is done to the fig tree, but also if ye shall say unto this mountain, Be thou removed, and be thou cast into the sea; it shall be done.* ___And all things, whatsoever ye shall ask in prayer, believing, ye shall receive.___*" (Matt. 21:21-22)*

I've heard some people say that since no good thing is within us, (Rom. 7:18), then doing good deeds is meaningless because the Lord has given us all these things to begin with. According to them, this would be like repaying a debt to someone by borrowing the money from them. No, not quite. It's more like returning the money originally borrowed. The Lord supplies every Christian with a certain amount of talents and he is expected to utilize them fully and wisely. *"For unto whomsoever much is given, of him shall be much required"* (Luke 12:48). That's why we were given them in the first place; this is our *"___duty___"* as Christians, (Luke 17:7-10). If we are blessed with a strong body we need to help the weak. If we are blessed with good health we should help the sick. If we possess wealth we should help the poor; and so on. All these gifts are not given to us to keep to ourselves; but they have been "loaned" to us. Christ requires that we return them and we do so by doing good works for others, (Matt. 25:31-46). It is important to understand that although Christians cannot "earn" the Kingdom of Heaven by doing good deeds, (Rom. 4:1-5), they very possibly could earn exclusion from it by failing to do them, (cf. Matt. 7:24-27; 21:28-31; Luke 6:47-49). If we fail to utilize our talents and *"bury them in the sand,"* whether out of greed, pride, laziness, or any other reason, we will be held accountable. Otherwise, we make a contradiction of the New Testament because there is absolutely no doubt that Christ and the Apostles both commanded that we abstain from sin and perform good deeds. These things all come together to complete the task of salvation, *"Seest thou how faith wrought with his works, and by works was faith made perfect?"* (James 2:22).

Some might contend that good works will naturally proceed from a true Christian. This is only half true. Many Christians have used this logic to excuse laziness and only do that which is convenient. This is inadequate; we need to "go the extra mile". Like the widow who put her entire living into the collection box as opposed to those who put in much more but only out of convenience. We all need to pull ourselves off the soft cushions of complacency and do some work. Happy is the Christian who is doing these things and not just hearing them!

Now I'm not trying to frighten you or rock the foundations of your faith. Neither am I attempting to place heavy burdens upon you. I am going to be judged by these standards too. So what does all this boil down to? Simply this: If we believe Christ died and rose again for the remission of sins and are utilizing our God-given gifts, and are trying our best not to sin, we've nothing to fear. If, on the other hand, we believe in the atoning death and resurrection of our Lord Jesus Christ and are not utilizing our God-given talents, and are not trying our best to abstain from sin, we do have something to fear. Yes, sin is inherent within us and we cannot overcome it altogether no matter how hard we try, (Rom. 7:13-25). But we shouldn't use that as an excuse to just give in to sin or quit trying not to sin. It also doesn't mean that we should become lazy or just sit back complacently and stop doing good works for others even (or especially) if they are inconvenient. This is where judgment comes into play. Only the Lord can draw the line between what is acceptable and what is unacceptable. Only the Lord knows whether we tried our best or not.

I have many more things I'd like to say concerning antinomianism, predestination, the free will of man, and justification. But time and space does not afford me the luxury of doing so at this time. There's no doubt that this is an important and neglected issue and there's definitely a need for a book dealing specifically with it. But I need to keep focused on my main mission of confuting the pretribulation rapture and millennial concepts. For all intents and purposes however, at least for my needs here, I feel I've addressed these issues sufficiently. I'm sure that if my readers take the time to research the passages I've cited they'll see the truth of this matter.

CHAPTER TWO

THE PRETRIBULATION RAPTURE

I will now briefly define a few terms I will be mentioning throughout the course of this disquisition. They are as follows:

(A). "Tribulation: Great misery or distress, as from oppression; deep sorrow. Something that causes suffering or distress; affliction, trial." (Webster's New World Dictionary)

The Holy Bible warns of an approaching "Tribulation period". In other words, a time of peril, distress, and trial. The tribulations we're concerned with here are those directly connected to and preceding the Second Advent of our Lord Jesus Christ, (See Matt. 24, Mark 13, and Luke 21). In these passages Jesus explains that a period of trial and anguish will transpire just before His Second Coming. Many Bible teachers refer to this period of time as "the great tribulation period" or "the seven-year tribulation period".

Many scholars agree that this period of trial and distress will prevail for seven years. But that assumption is not necessarily correct. The notion that this tribulation period will endure for exactly seven years is (or could be) a matter of debate. Such ideas were derived from personal interpretations of the Holy Scriptures, namely, Daniel's vision of the seventy weeks, (Dan. 9:24-27). I agree it is educated guesswork, but guesswork nonetheless. Inferences are not worthy of whole-hearted belief. There are good Christians who agree with this theory, and there are others who disagree. In both cases, the chance of being incorrect remains a possibility. Therefore, such ideas cannot be seriously considered without some degree of skepticism. The tribulation might be a longer, or shorter period of time than these scholars anticipate.

(B). "Rapture: The state of being carried away with joy, love etc. An expression of great joy, pleasure, etc. A carrying away or being carried away in body or spirit." (Webster's New World Dictionary)

First of all, the word 'rapture' cannot be found within the Bible. Many Bible teachers profess that Christ will snatch away (or rapture) His elect from the earth either before or in the middle of the great tribulation period. According to their teachings, Christ will return invisibly and rescue His chosen ones from this awful period of trial by rapturing them up into the Kingdom of Heaven. This means that Christians will be exempt from these adversities because they will not even be here on earth when they come to pass.

(C). Millennium: Since the rapture and millennial concepts are so closely connected and/or related, it will be almost impossible to completely separate them. Hence, I will provide a brief denotation for the term now. Again, the actual word 'millennium' is not in the Bible. It is a Latin word signifying the number 1,000. When this term is applied to Biblical prophecy, it designates the thousand-year reign described in the Twentieth Chapter of the Book of Revelation.

Certain people of today are "suggesting" that there will be a millennium (or 1,000 years) of peace and tranquility upon this planet. In addition, they are claiming that Jesus Christ Himself will be King and Ruler upon this earth during this alleged thousand-year theocracy. Needless to say, I do not agree with this opinion. This idea gives false christs a superb opportunity to emerge. But I will not discuss this idea with great detail right now. I just want my readers to have a basic understanding of the term for the few times they may encounter it within these chapters about the rapture. For the most part, I intend to keep these two ideas separate. But there will be times when I will be forced to mention the millennium. This is because many rapture teachers advocate both of these theories. Many of them claim that Christ returns invisibly to rapture His elect before the tribulation period, and then after this period of adversity expires, Jesus returns again with His previously raptured chosen ones in His Second Coming, and this is when He begins His millennial reign upon earth. These individuals may not realize it yet, but these two ideas contradict one another, and when appropriate, I will point this out. Otherwise, I will do my best to keep them apart.

Indeed, there is a rapture of sorts spoken of within Scripture.

Christ will take up, or rapture, His Church at the end of the present dispensation. St. Paul wrote about this great event in his First Epistle to the Thessalonians:

"For the Lord himself shall descend from heaven with a shout, with the voice of the archangel, and with the trump(et) of God: and the dead in Christ shall rise first: Then we which are alive and remain shall be caught up (Raptured) together with them in the clouds, to meet the Lord in the air: and so shall we ever be with the Lord. Wherefore comfort one another with these words." (I Thess. 4:16-18)

That passage unquestionably implicates a type of rapture. I support that position without protest. However, the question isn't whether or not it will transpire. It is rather, **when** will it occur? Answers to this are classified into three beliefs. Those beliefs, in relation to the Second Advent of Christ, are as follows:

(I). Pretribulation View: This theory portrays Jesus returning **invisibly** to rapture His chosen ones into Heaven **before** the great tribulation period. According to this view, nobody will witness this spectacular event. These individuals will simply disappear from the face of the earth; cars will go careening off highways as their drivers are taken up, airplanes will come crashing down as pilots get snatched out of cockpits, etc. Those who were not "worthy" to participate in the rapture will be left behind to endure the tribulation period. Then after this period of adversity expires, those who were previously raptured will return with Christ in His Second Coming.

This theory is the one I intend to confute. It is, by far, the most hazardous of the three. Whenever you encounter anything indicative of the rapture within this book, it is the pretribulation theory I am referring to.

(II). Midtribulation View: This theory holds that Jesus will return to rapture His Church in the **middle** of the great tribulation period. Then, after three and one-half years, Jesus' Second Coming takes place.

Not unlike the pretribulation view, this opinion is deleterious as well. But it isn't nearly as dangerous. Since nobody knows when

Christ is coming, (Matt. 24:36), then it essentially follows that it would be impossible to determine whether or not we were in the middle of the tribulation period. This would be true even assuming this period of oppression will endure for precisely seven years. Because to place a definite date on the middle of the tribulation period places a definite date on both its beginning and ending. Which, in turn, fixes a definite date on Christ's Second Coming. Since these calculations cannot be made with certainty, it is not necessary to discuss this theory with great detail. These individuals could be waiting on this rapture right up to Christ's Second Coming, which makes this viewpoint redundant.

(III). Posttribulation View: This particular theory maintains that the rapture and Christ's return are one and the same event. In other words, Christ does not come back for His Church until His Second Advent.

The Posttribulation View virtually coincides with my convictions. I believe Christians will be alive and present upon the earth when these trials come to pass. I do not believe they will be taken into the Kingdom of God, or anywhere else, during this time of trouble. The only aspect of this idea with which I would disagree is if the notion of an upcoming millennial reign upon this earth were tacked onto it. Otherwise, this view is scripturally sound.

CHAPTER THREE

CHRISTIANS IN TRIBULATION

It seems to me that advocates of this rapture are beginning to realize just how terrible the tribulation period could be. They seem to be frantically searching Scripture for something that simply is not there. It appears as though these individuals are looking for a way to circumvent this period of trial. But should we completely overlook or ignore the fact that it is tribulation which separates the true Christians from the false Christians?

God's elect are exposed to trials and tribulations to teach them trust, patience, obedience, and longanimity. Evidence for this can be found throughout the entire Bible. In the Old Testament, God would often teach the Children of Israel these things with the many battles they had against their hostile neighbors. Victory or defeat was determined by whether or not Israel obeyed God's Commandments. When they were obedient to His Holy Commandments, they were rewarded with victory. They would enjoy peace and prosperity for as long as they maintained this manner of living. But when the Children of Israel would reject the Lord and disobey His statutes, they would suffer defeat at the hands of their enemies. This punishment would continue for as long as they refused to do the Will of God. Their men of war would die by the sword, their cities would be destroyed, the survivors would be led into captivity, and their women would be ravished, (See Lev. 26:1-46; Deut. 4:25-31; Judges 3:8-10; Neh. 1:8-9). Evidence for this fact is so extensive that if I attempted to list all the relevant Scriptures, I'd be forced to rewrite virtually the entire Old Testament. But since the Promises of God no longer pertain to a single nation only, this method of reward and punishment cannot be utilized expediently anymore. This is because Christians are not centralized or concentrated into a limited area as the Children of Israel were.

It is crucial that my readers understand that tests, trials, adversities, tribulations, oppression, persecutions, afflictions, etc. do, and will continue to occur in the lives of God's faithful servants. This is particularly true for Christians since the old methods of correction are no longer efficacious. It is also important to remember that the sins of Israel were more of a physical nature than those of Christians. For example: In the Old Testament, committing adultery was a sin. But in the New Testament, <u>thinking</u> of committing adultery is just as sinful as actually doing it, (Matt. 5:27-28). Therefore, many of sin's aftereffects we experience as Christians are inward and spiritual in nature. That's why a "new" and "better" sacrifice was needed; the body of our Lord Jesus Christ. The blood of bulls and goats etc. could not bring about a clear conscience, (Heb. 9:9-14; 10:1-18). I suspect that many of the most serious sins we as Christians commit are of the mind rather than the physical body. This can sometimes make them difficult to recognize, and a lot easier to disguise, even from our own selves. Pride, self-pity, vanity, complacency, lust, overconfidence, jealousy, envy, hatred, prejudice, and self-righteousness are all sins of the mind. These are not always easy for us to perceive and we would be in danger of taking them all the way to the grave, if it weren't for trials and tribulations to point them out and humble us. Hence, physical tribulation is designed to correct the spiritual person. We must rely solely upon our faith and the Holy Spirit to overcome these adversities. In so doing, we attain true righteousness. As it is written in Scripture:

" *If ye endure chastening, God dealeth with you as with sons;* ***For what son is he whom the father chasteneth not?*** *But if ye be without chastisement, whereof all are partakers, then are ye bastards, and not sons. Furthermore we have had fathers of our flesh which corrected us, and we gave them reverence: shall we not much rather be in subjection unto the father of spirits, and live? For they verily for a few days chastened us after their own pleasure;* ***But he for our profit, that we might be partakers of his holiness.*** *Now no chastening for the present seemeth to be joyous, but grievous: nevertheless afterward* ***it yieldeth the peaceable fruit of righteousness unto them*** *which are exercised thereby." (Heb. 12:7-11).*

Since the whole idea behind the pretribulation theory is to escape physical suffering, I will approach this topic aggressively and exhaustively. I will now provide a rather expansive list of Scriptural passages which show that trials and tribulations always have, do now, and always will take place in the lives of God's chosen ones. I will focus primarily upon the New Testament. But I will list a few Old Testament passages in order to prove my point. I will underline the specific example regarding the test. When a reason for the test or trial is given, or the reasoning behind it, I will both underline it and put the text in **bold** print. Listen to the Word of the Lord God:

*"And it came to pass after these things, that God did tempt (or test) Abraham, and said unto him, Abraham: and he said, Behold, here I am. And he said, Take now thy son, thine only son Isaac, whom thou lovest, and get thee into the land of Moriah; and offer him there for a burnt offering upon one of the mountains which I will tell thee of... And Abraham stretched forth his hand, and took the knife to slay his son. And the angel of the Lord called unto him out of heaven, and said, Abraham, Abraham: and he said, Here am I. And he said, Lay not thine hand upon the lad, neither do thou anything unto him: **For now I know that thou fearest God,** seeing thou hast not withheld thy son, thine only son from me." (Gen. 22:1-2, 10-12).*

*"Then said the Lord unto Moses, Behold, I will rain bread from heaven for you; and the people shall go out and gather a certain rate every day, that I may prove them, **whether they will walk in my way, or no**." (Ex. 16:4).*

*"And they said unto Moses, Speak thou with us, and we will hear: but let not God speak with us, lest we die. And Moses said unto the people, Fear not: for God has come to prove you, **that his fear may be before your faces, that ye sin not**" (Ex. 20:19-20).*

*"When thou art in tribulation, and all these things are come upon thee, even in the latter days, **if thou turn to the Lord thy God, and shalt be obedient unto his voice**; (For the Lord thy God is a merciful God;) **he will not forsake thee, neither destroy thee**, nor forget the*

covenant of thy fathers which he sware unto them." (Deut. 4:30-31).

"*And thou shalt remember all the way which the Lord thy God led thee these forty years in the wilderness, to hunble thee, and to prove thee, to know what was in thine heart, whether thou wouldest keep his commandments, or no… Who fed thee in the wilderness with manna, which thy fathers knew not, that he might humble thee, and that he might prove thee, to do thee good at thy latter end;" (Deut. 8:2, 16).*

"*Thou shalt not hearken unto the words of that prophet, or that dreamer of dreams: for the Lord your God proveth you, to know whether ye love the Lord your God with all your heart and with all your soul." (Deut. 13:3).*

"*I also will not henceforth drive out any from before them of the nations which Joshua left when he died: That through them I may prove Israel, whether they will keep the way of the Lord to walk therein, as their fathers did keep it, or not." (Judges 2:21-22).*

"*Now these are the nations which the Lord left, to prove Israel by them, even as many of Israel as had not known all the wars of Canaan;… And they were to prove Israel by them, to know whether they would hearken unto the commandments of the Lord, which he commanded their fathers by the hand of Moses." (Judges 3:1, 4)*

"*Howbeit in the business of the ambassadors of the princes of Babylon, who sent unto him to inquire of the wonder that was done in the land, God left him, to try him, that he might know all that was in his heart." (II Chr. 32:31)*

"*Behold, happy is the man whom God correcteth, therefore despise not thou the chastening of the Almighty: for he maketh sore, and he bindeth up: he woundeth, and his hands make whole." (Job 5:17-18).*

"*The Lord is in his holy temple, the Lord's throne is in heaven: his eyes behold, his eyelids try, the children of men. The Lord trieth the righteous: but the wicked and him that loveth violence his soul hateth." (Psa. 11:4-5).*

"*O bless our God, ye people, and make the voice of his praise to be heard: which holdeth our soul in life, and suffereth not our feet to* *be moved. For thou, O God, <u>hast proved us</u>: <u>thou hast tried us</u>, as silver is tried. Thou broughtest us into the net; <u>thou laidest affliction upon our loins</u>. Thou hast caused men to ride over our heads; we went through fire and through water: <u>**But thou broughtest us out into a wealthy place**</u>." (Psa. 66:8-12).*

"But, O Lord of hosts, <u>that triest the righteous</u>, and seest the reins of the heart, let me see thy vengeance on them: for unto thee have I opened my cause." (Jer. 20:12).

*"And I will bring the third part through the fire, and will refine them as silver is refined, <u>and will try them as gold is tried</u>: <u>**They shall call on my name, and I will hear them**</u>: I will say, It is my people: and they shall say, The Lord is my God." (Zech. 13:9).*

This list could go on and on. The trials and tribulations of the Old Testament are well documented. I suppose a fair-sized book could be written on this topic alone. There's Adam and the forbidden fruit, Noah and the flood, Lot in Sodom and Gomorrah, Joseph sold into slavery, Isaarel's hard bondage in Egypt, Moses and Pharaoh, the Exodus from Egypt, Israel's 40 years of wandering in the desert, Samson captured by the Philistines and his eyes put out, David and Goliath, the prophet Jeremiah imprisoned, Daniel in the lion's den, Jonah and the Whale, Israel's long captivity in Babylon, etc. Many of the greatest stories of the Old Testament are about mere men overcoming insurmountable obstacles by the power of God Almighty. The entire book of Job is dedicated to the sufferings of the righteous and how they ought to respond to them.

This did not change at all when Christ came. In fact, the New Testament is replete with warnings about Christians suffering tests, trials, and tribulations. Take your time and read the following examples very carefully:

*"<u>Blessed are ye which are persecuted for righteousness' sake</u>: for theirs is the kingdom of heaven. Blessed are ye, when men shall revile you, and persecute you, and shall say all manner of evil against you falsely for my sake. Rejoice, and be exceeding glad: <u>**For great is your reward in heaven**</u>: <u>**For so persecuted they the prophets which were before you**</u>." (Matt. 5:10-12).*

*"But I say unto you, Love your enemies, bless them that curse you, do good to them that hate you, and pray for them that despitefully use you, <u>and persecute you</u>; <u>**that ye may be the children of your Father which is in heaven**</u>: for he maketh his sun to rise on the evil and on the good, and sendeth rain on the just and on the unjust."* (Matt. 5:44-45).

"And ye shall be hated of all men for my name's sake: <u>But he that shall endure unto the end, the same shall be saved</u>." (Mark 13:13).

*"Blessed are ye, when men shall hate you, and when they shall separate you from their company, and shall reproach you, and cast out your name as evil, for the Son of man's sake. Rejoice ye in that day, and leap for joy: For, behold, <u>**your reward is great in heaven**</u>."* (Luke 6:22-23).

*"Remember the word that I said unto you, the servant is not greater than his lord. <u>**If they have persecuted me**, they also will persecute you</u>."* (John 15:20).

"These things have I spoken unto you, <u>that in me ye might have peace. In the world ye shall have tribulation: But be of good cheer; I have overcome the world</u>." (John 16:33).

"And to him they agreed: and when they had called the Apostles, <u>and beaten them</u>, they commanded that they should not speak in the name of Jesus, and let them go. And they departed from the presence of the council, <u>rejoicing that they were accounted worthy to suffer shame for his name</u>." (Acts 5:40-41).

"Confirming the souls of the disciples, and exhorting them to continue in the faith, <u>and that we must through much tribulation enter the kingdom of God</u>." (Acts 14:22)

"And now, behold, I go bound in the spirit unto Jerusalem, not knowing the things that shall befall me there: Save that the Holy Ghost witnesseth in every city, saying that <u>bonds and afflictions abide me</u>. But none of these things move me, neither count I my life dear unto myself, so that I might finish my course with joy, and the ministry, which I have received of the Lord Jesus, to testify the gospel of the grace of God." (Acts 20:22-24).

*"And not only so, <u>but we glory in tribulations also: **Knowing**</u>*

that tribulation worketh patience;" (Rom. 5:3).

"And if children, then heirs, heirs of God, and joint-heirs with Christ; if so be that we suffer with him, that we may be also glorified together... Who shall separate us from the love of Christ? Shall tribulation, or distress, or persecution, or famine, or nakedness, or peril, or sword? For thy sake we are killed all the day long; we are accounted as sheep for the slaughter." (Rom. 8:17, 35-36).

"Even unto this present hour we both hunger, and thirst, and are naked, and are buffeted, and have no certain dwelling place; And labor, working with our own hands: being reviled, we bless; being persecuted, we suffer it: Being defamed, we entreat: We are made as the filth of the world, and are the offscouring of all things unto this day. I write not these things to shame you, but as my beloved sons I warn you." (I Cor. 4:11-14)

"Blessed be God, even the Father of our Lord Jesus Christ, the Father of mercies, and the God of all comfort; Who comforteth us in all our tribulation, that we may be able to comfort them which are in any trouble, by the comfort wherewith we ourselves are comforted of God. For as the sufferings of Christ abound in us, so our consolation also aboundeth by Christ." (II Cor. 1:3-5).

"We are troubled on every side, yet not distressed; we are perplexed, but not in despair; Persecuted, but not forsaken; cast down, but not destroyed; Always bearing about in the body the dying of the Lord Jesus, that the life also of Jesus might be made manifest in our body. For we which live are always delivered unto death for Jesus' sake, that the life also of Jesus might be made manifest in our mortal flesh." (II Cor. 4:8-11).

"For which cause we faint not, but though our outward man perish, yet the inward man is renewed day by day. For our light affliction, which is but for a moment, worketh for us a far more exceeding and eternal weight of glory." (II Cor. 4:16-17).

"But in all things approving ourselves as the ministers of God, in much patience, in afflictions, in necessities, in distress, In stripes, in imprisonments, in tumults, in labors, in watchings, in fastings; By pureness, by knowledge, by long-suffering, by kindness, by the Holy

Ghost, by love unfeigned." (II Cor.6:4-6).

"Great is my boldness of speech toward you, great is my glorying of you: I am filled with comfort, <u>I am exceeding joyful in all our tribulation</u>." (II Cor. 7:4).

*"Moreover, brethren, we do you to wit of the grace of God bestowed on the churches of Macedonia; How <u>that in a great trial of affliction</u> the abundance of their joy and their deep poverty <u>**abounded unto the riches of their liberality**</u>." (II Cor. 8:1-2).*

*"Therefore I take pleasure in <u>infirmities</u>, in <u>reproaches</u>, in <u>necessities</u>, in <u>persecutions</u>, in <u>distresses</u>, for Christ's sake: <u>**For when I am weak, then am I strong**</u>." (II Cor. 12:10).*

*"<u>**For unto you it is given in the behalf of Christ, not only to believe on him,**</u> but <u>also to suffer for his sake</u>." (Phil. 1:29).*

"For ye, brethren, became followers of the churches of God which in Judea are in Christ Jesus: <u>for ye also have suffered</u> like things of your own countrymen, even as they have of the Jews: Who both killed the Lord Jesus, and their own prophets, and <u>have persecuted us</u>, and they please not God, and are contrary to all men:" (I Thess. 2:14-15).

*"<u>That no man should be moved by these afflictions: **For yourselves know that we are appointed thereunto**</u>. For verily, when we were with you, we told you before <u>that we should suffer tribulation</u>; even as it came to pass, and ye know." (I Thess. 3:3-4).*

*"So that we ourselves glory in you in the churches of God for your patience and faith <u>in all your persecutions and tribulations that ye endure: **which is a manifest token of the righteous judgment of God, that ye may be accounted worthy of the kingdom of God**, for which ye also suffer</u>." (II Thess. 1:4-5).*

"Be not thou therefore ashamed of the testimony of our Lord, nor of me his prisoner: <u>but be thou partaker of the afflictions</u> of the gospel according to the power of God;" (II Tim. 1:8).

*"Yea, and <u>**all that will live godly in Christ Jesus**</u> shall suffer <u>tribulation</u>." (II Tim. 3:12).*

*"But watch thou in all things, <u>endure afflictions</u>, do the work of an evangelist, <u>**make full proof of thy ministry**</u>." (II Tim. 4:5).*

"*But call to remembrance the former days, in which, after ye were illuminated, ye endured a great fight of afflictions; Partly, whilst ye were made a gazingstock both by reproaches and afflictions; and partly, whilst ye became companions of them that were so used.*" *(Heb. 10:32-33).*

"*By faith Moses, when he was come to years, refused to be called the son of Pharaoh's daughter; Choosing rather to suffer affliction with the people of God, than to enjoy the pleasures of sin for a season; Esteeming the reproach of Christ greater riches than the treasures of Egypt: for he had respect unto the recompense of the reward.*" *(Heb. 11:24-26).*

"*My brethren, count it all joy when ye fall into divers temptations; Knowing this, that the trying of your faith worketh patience.*" *(James 1:2-3).*

"*Blessed is the man that endureth temptation: for when he is tried, he shall receive the crown of life, which the Lord hath promised to them that love him.*" *(James 1:12).*

"*Take, my brethren, the prophets, who have spoken in the name of the Lord, for an example for suffering affliction, and of patience. Behold, we count them happy which endure. Ye have heard of the patience of Job, and have seen the end of the Lord; that the Lord is very pitiful, and of tender mercy.*" *(James 5:10-11).*

"*Wherein ye greatly rejoice, though now for a season, if need be, ye are in heaviness through manifold temptations: That the trial of your faith, being much more precious than of gold that perisheth, though it be tried with fire, might be found unto praise and honor and glory at the appearing of Jesus Christ:*" *(I Pet. 1:6-7).*

"*For what glory is it, if, when ye be buffeted for your faults, ye shall take it patiently? but if, when ye do well, and suffer for it, ye take it patiently, this is acceptable with God. For even hereunto were ye called: because Christ also suffered for us, leaving us an example, that ye should follow his steps:*" *(I Pet. 2:20-21).*

"*But and if ye suffer for righteousness' sake, happy are ye: and be not afraid of their terror, neither be troubled; ... For it is better, if the will of God be so, that ye suffer for well doing, than for evil* doing." (I Pet. 3:14, 17).

"Beloved, think it not strange concerning the fiery trial which is to try you, as though some strange thing happened unto you: But rejoice, inasmuch as ye are partakers of Christ's sufferings; that, when his glory shall be revealed, ye may be glad also with exceeding joy. If ye be reproached for the name of Christ, **happy are ye; for the spirit of glory and of God resteth upon you**: on their part he is evil spoken of, but on your part he is glorified. But let none of you suffer as a murderer, or as a thief, or as an evildoer, or as a busybody in other men's matters. Yet if any man suffer as a Christian, let him not be ashamed; **But let him glorify God on his behalf.** For the time is come that judgment must begin at the house of God: and if it first begin at us, what shall the end be of them that obey not the gospel of God? And if the righteous scarcely be saved, where shall the ungodly and the sinner appear? Wherefore let them that suffer **according to the will of God** commit the keeping of their souls to him in well doing, as unto a faithful Creator." (I Pet. 4:12-19).

"Be sober, be vigilant; because your adversary the Devil, as a roaring lion, walketh about, seeking whom he may devour: Whom resist steadfast in the faith, knowing that the same afflictions are accomplished in your brethren that are in the world. But the God of all grace, who hath called us unto his eternal glory by Christ Jesus, after ye have suffered a while, **make you perfect, stablish, strengthen, settle you.**" (I Pet. 5:8-10).

"I know thy works, and tribulation, and poverty, (but thou art rich) and I know the blasphemy of them which say they are Jews, and are not, but are the synagogue of Satan. Fear none of those things which thou shalt suffer: behold, the devil shall cast some of you into prison, that ye may be tried; and ye shall have tribulation ten days, be thou faithful unto death, **and I will give thee a crown of life.**" (Rev. 2:9-10).

And there are more passages that could be added to this list. I didn't want to weary you. If any more time and space were dedicated to this topic within the New Testament, there wouldn't be much room left to address the main reason it was written. Consider Jesus Christ

Himself: Why was He led by the Spirit of God into the wilderness before He began His ministry? Jesus spent forty days in the wilderness being tempted by Satan. It wasn't until He refused the power and wealth of the entire world that Satan finally left Him, (See Matt. 4:1-11; Mark 1:12-13; Luke 4:1-13). The Scriptures state that Jesus was tested like us in every way:

*"Seeing then that we have a great high priest, that is passed into the heavens, Jesus the Son of God, let us hold fast our profession. For we have not a high priest which cannot be touched with the feeling of our infirmities; **But was in all points tempted like as we are**, yet without sin. " (Heb. 4:14-15).*

It was imperative that Christ experience sufferings and temptations of the flesh so that He could assist us in our varied trials and tribulations. As it is written:

*"But we see Jesus, who was made a little lower than the angels for the suffering of death, crowned with glory and honor; that he by the grace of God should taste death for every man. For it became him, for whom are all things, and by whom are all things, in bringing many sons unto glory, **to make the captain of their salvation perfect through sufferings**... Wherefore in all things it behooved him to be made like unto his brethren, **that he might be a merciful and faithful high priest in things pertaining to God**, to make reconciliation for the sins of the people. **For in that he himself hath suffered being tempted, he is able to succor (assist) them that are tempted.**" (Heb. 2:9-10, 17-18). See also Heb. 5:8; Luke 22:28.*

We as Christians must understand that God uses these trials and tribulations to refine us, purify us, sanctify us, and separate the true Christians from the false Christians. If the person evades the trial, then he is a coward and is not a true Christian. But if the person confronts the trial with patience, trust, and forbearance, he is a true Christian indeed. The Bible states that fact apodictically. Anyone can claim to be a Christian when there are no undesirable circumstances to think about. Anyone can claim they would lay down their life for Christ when their head is not on the guillotine. But a true Christian would remain steadfast in his faith no matter what the circumstances or consequences might be. Tribulation can only strengthen a true believer. But a false Christian is crushed to pieces thereby, (cf. Matt. 13:20-21). As it is spoken by our Lord:

*"And these are they likewise which are sown on stony ground; who, when they have heard the word, immediately receive it with gladness; And have no root in themselves, and so endure for a time: afterward, **when affliction or persecution ariseth for the word's sake, immediately they are offended.**"* (Mark 4:16-17)

We notice from many of the aforementioned excerpts that if we endure trials and adversities, our *"reward is great in heaven"*. Have you ever seen anyone receive a reward for doing something that was easy or ordinary? Rewards are never given for nothing. They are given to someone for doing that which is difficult. *"Because strait is the gate, and narrow is the way, which leadeth unto life, and few there be that find it."* (Matt. 7:14). Now if we attempt to evade our trials what sort of reward should we expect? (For further references about these rewards, see: Matt. 6:1-18; 10:41-42; Mark 9:41; Luke 6:35; I Cor. 3:8, 14; 9:17-18; I Tim. 5:18; Heb. 11:6; II John 8; Rev. 11:18; 22:12). I've devoted a great deal of attention to this topic in Chapter One.

Now for the sake of argument: Let's suppose Christians were raptured before this period of oppression. How could this be fair to those who endured great suffering and distress for Christ's sake in times past? My conviction is this: If anyone was "worthy" enough to be spared of these hardships, the Apostles were more so than any of us. Were they excluded though? Of course not. They were homeless, hungry, cold, persecuted, tortured, spit upon, humiliated, ridiculed, beaten, whipped, ostracized, and forsaken by their friends and family. They were robbed and betrayed by their fellow workers. They suffered loneliness, nakedness, and fear. Finally, they were executed for the Holy Name of Jesus Christ. Should we consider ourselves "better" or more righteous than they? Just think what would've happened to Christianity if the Apostles believed they were going to get raptured!

Now consider all the good Christians who have died in the past of terrible debilitating diseases such as cancer or AIDS. These individuals often suffer excruciating pain for several years. Why weren't they raptured? Consider all the Christians who have died by electrocution, car accidents, drownings, fires, etc. Why weren't they spared? Consider all the good Christians who have suffered great mental anguish by rape, child abuse, or the loss of a child by kidnapping: Why weren't they translated? How about those who are confined to a wheelchair because they have lost several limbs, or perhaps, they are paralyzed due to disease or nerve damage? Why are they left behind? What about the small child who must endure a lifetime of shame because her face has been scarred by fire? Why didn't she get raptured? How about all the prophets of the Old Testament? Why were they left in constant despair and disconsolation? How about Jesus Christ and John the Baptist? Why were they executed? How about all the good Christians who were mercilessly slaughtered by the heathen Roman Empire? Why were they deprived of a pretribulation rapture? Thousands of Christians were beheaded, crucified, thrown to the lions, and burned at the stake for the Roman's entertainment! Is it even possible to fathom how terrifying that must have been? Can we imagine what it's like being thrown into the arena facing these hungry lions knowing full well what their intentions were? Or can we imagine what it's like being tied to a stake and having flames of fire licking at our feet? I wonder what it's like walking up to the guillotine and voluntarily placing your head on it!

Many of those early Christians could have avoided these cruel executions if only they would have denied Christ and given homage to Caesar. Those early persecutions were necessary for a "testimony" against the heathen Roman society and its tyranical rulers. Our present-day society is no better than it was back then. In my opinion it is far worse. My reader merely has to take a glance out his window or at his television to see that I speak the truth. Our current living conditions are like those of Sodom and Gomorrah, Babylon, Nineveh, and Rome combined. Vanity, drugs, drunkenness, pornography, lust, greed, pride, murder, robbery, adultery, envy, hatred, jealousy, blasphemy, godlessness, debauchery, rape, homosexuality, beastiality, child abuse, disrespect, hypocrisy, racism, laziness, gluttony, revenge, and falsehood abound in our streets. These are all signs of the end times, (See I Tim. 4:1-3 and II Tim. 3:1-9). Yes, most definitely, a testimony may be required of us as well.

Now let us look at this retrospectively and reason together. If all of God's elect were exposed to trials and tribulations from the beginning of time until now, then why should Christians of today expect to be treated any differently? The answer is that we shouldn't expect to be spared of any more hardships than anyone else. All of this happens because trust, patience, and endurance are integral parts of being Christian. If a person is a true Christian, then there's a very strong possibility that his faith may be tried and he may have to suffer sometime during his lifetime. Why do you think we are warned of these things so frequently within the Bible?

The main goal of this chapter was to show that trials and tribulations always have, do now, and always will take place in the lives of God's faithful servants. That being established I will now proceed to the next phase of my argument.

CHAPTER FOUR

FALSE DOCTRINE AND THE WRATH OF GOD

Like I said in Chapter One, many people are under the impression that just because Christians "*are not appointed to wrath,*" it is only logical that they should be spared the tribulation period. I've heard this time and time again. Let me elucidate one thing right now: There's a big difference between God's wrath and tribulation. God's wrath is righteous anger and implies eternal punishment; repentance and forgiveness are no longer options, (John 3:36; Heb. 10:30-31). A person can have the wrath of God abide on him and he may never even know it or experience tribulation in his lifetime. Many rich and wicked individuals have lived and died without ever experiencing tribulation or the wrath of God. But God often uses tribulation to correct His beloved children as we've seen in the preceding chapter, (cf. I Cor. 11:32). We need to keep in mind what the wrath of God is and who it is directed toward. The wrath of God is not only reserved for wicked unbelievers. God hates false doctrine and His wrath abides on all those who preach or follow it. And when we stray from the truth we put ourselves in danger of believing lies:

"***Let no man deceive you with vain words: For because of these things cometh the wrath of God upon the children of disobedience***. *Be not ye therefore partakers with them.*" *(Eph. 5:6-7)*

"*And with all deceivableness of unrighteousness in them that perish;* ***because they received not the love of the truth****, that they might be saved.* ***And for this cause God shall send them strong delusion, that they should believe a lie: That they all might be damned who believed not the truth****, but had pleasure in unrighteousness.*" *(II Thess. 2:10-12)*

"*For therein is the righteousness of God revealed from faith to faith: as it is written, The just shall live by faith.* ***For the wrath of God is revealed from heaven against all ungodliness and*** *__unrighteousness__ __of__ __men__, __who__ hold __the__ __truth__ in __unrighteousness__; Because that which may be known of God is manifest in them; for God hath shown it unto them. For the invisible things of him from the creation of the world __are__ __clearly__ __seen__, being understood by the things that are made, even his eternal power and Godhead; __so__ __that__ __they__ __are__ __without__ __excuse__: Because that, when they knew God, they glorified him not as God, neither were thankful; __but__ __became__ __vain__ __in__ __their__ __imaginations__, __and__ __their__ __foolish__ __heart__ __was__ __darkened__. __Professing__ __themselves__ __to__ __be__ __wise__, __they__ __became__ __fools__,"* (Rom. 1:17-22) See also vv 24-25.

"But after thy hardness and impenitent heart __treasurest__ __up__ __unto__ __thyself__ __wrath__ __against__ __the__ __day__ __of__ __wrath__ and Revelation of the righteous judgment of God; Who will render to every man according to his deeds: To them who by patient continuance in well doing seek for glory and honor and immortality, eternal life: But unto them that are contentious, __and__ __do__ __not__ __obey__ __the__ __truth__, but obey unrighteousness, __indignation__ __and__ __wrath__, __tribulation__ __and__ __anguish__, upon every soul of man that doeth evil, of the Jew first, and also of the Gentile;" (Rom. 2:5-9)

"I marvel that ye are so soon removed from him that called you into the grace of Christ unto another gospel: Which is not another; __but__ __there__ __be__ __some__ __that__ __trouble__ __you__, __and__ __would__ __pervert__ __the__ __gospel__ __of__ __Christ__. But though we, or an angel from heaven, preach any other gospel unto you than that which we have preached unto you, __let__ __him__ __be__ __accursed__. As we said before, so say I now again, __If__ __any__ __man__ __preach__ __any__ __other__ __gospel__ __unto__ __you__ __than__ __that__ __ye__ __have__ __received__, __let__ __him__ __be__ __accursed__." (Gal. 1:6-9)

When Christians wander from the Truth, *"God shall send them strong delusion, that they should believe a lie"*. What a profound declaration! Could it be that belief in the very doctrine that Christians will be spared the tribulation period may be the very reason they won't? This is like looking at the truth in a mirror. The image appears veracious, but in reality it is an illusion because it is backward. Once a person believes a lie, it is very difficult for him to accept the truth again. The prophet Isaiah wrote:

*"He feedeth on ashes, **a deceived heart hath turned him aside**, that he cannot deliver his soul, nor say, Is there not a lie in my right hand?" (Isa. 44:20)*

Generally speaking, people are very reluctant to admit error. This is especially true of religious beliefs. But let's not be stubborn about this. After reading this book you will see that there's just too many problems with these theories to believe in them with all your heart. **You** are my motivation for writing this book. I am not trying to hurt your feelings. I don't want you to admit any error to me. Read this book with your heart open to God and He will walk you through it. If you sincerely ask Him to help you find the truth of this matter He will tenderly assist you.

False doctrine has become a huge problem in the Christian community. I see it everywhere I turn. The pretribulation rapture and millennial theories are two of these doctrines. The way in which innocent Christians have been offered these theories is the worst aspect of the problem. This is like being presented a poisonous substance on a silver platter. The concoction is enticing due to the manner in which it is introduced. Hence, the individual is deceived by outward appearances and gobbles down the lethal solution without hesitation. Solomon said:

"Bread of deceit is sweet to a man; but afterward his mouth shall be filled with gravel." (Prov. 20:17).

These two concepts are offered in a somewhat likewise manner. Educated Biblical scholars have advanced their pleasant-sounding and seemingly harmless theories to the Christian community. Many Christians have swallowed these ideas without a second thought because they appear logical and have been presented by learned men, (cf. Rom. 16:17-18; Col. 2:4-8). This is the very core of the problem. This is where danger lies and confusion begins. St. Paul warned the Ephesians of this:

*That we henceforth be no more children, tossed to and fro, **and carried about with every wind of doctrine**, by the sleight of men, and cunning craftiness, whereby they lie in wait to deceive;" (Eph. 4:14)*

Again, it is written:

*"**For the time will come when they will not endure sound doctrine**; but after their own lusts shall they heap to themselves teachers, having itching ears; And they shall turn away their ears from the truth, **and shall be turned unto fables**." (II Tim. 4:3-4)*

We shouldn't believe what we hear about the Bible simply because some well-known person told us or because it sounds logical. Many Bible teachers possess an unusual talent for advancing their opinions with such magniloquence and impetuosity that they produce a kind of "stupefacient" effect upon their audiences. I've often witnessed this myself in many religious circles; especially in TV evangelism. The audience seems to be so captivated by the speaker that the actual content of the speech given doesn't seem to matter much. It seems the message being advanced is almost universally accepted as truth without question.

As convincing as they might be, it is mandatory that we maintain open minds and carefully scrutinize every single thing we see or hear regarding scripture. It is important to remember that there were learned scriptural scholars in Christ's time just as there is now in our time. These scholars are referred to in the Bible as *"scribes and Pharisees"*. Due to their intense study and dedication, many people were inclined to believe their erroneous teachings, (cf. I Tim. 1:4, 7; 6:20-21) without question, resulting in their own demise, (Matt. 23:13-15; Luke 11:52). This is precisely what is happening today.

Now I don't want my readers to misunderstand my intentions. I am not saying that all these teachers do these things deliberately. Perhaps they don't fully realize how important this is. On the other hand, I am not entitled to say that these people are not purposely doing these things either. I am not attempting to condemn anyone. Neither am I attempting to exonerate anyone. Who am I that I should judge? No, God forbid that I judge another. But let us all be the judge of our own selves. As it is written in Scripture:

"Examine yourselves, whether ye be in the faith; prove your own selves. Know ye not your own selves, how that Jesus Christ is in you, except ye be reprobates?" (II Cor. 13:5)

Again, it is written:

"Beloved, if our heart condemn us not, then have we confidence toward God." (I John 3:21)

Understand therefore, that it is not important to know whether these individuals do these things purposely or not. The fact of the matter is that they're being done. Like I said before, all I'm trying to do is alert people to the inherent dangers of these concepts. And further, it is my sincere hope that the individuals who espouse these ideas take a very serious look at this and ponder the evidence put forth within. I want these people to realize that their opinions are now accepted by a vast and growing number of Christians as completely valid doctrine, worthy of unwavering belief.

Theories are theories. They are not fact. Otherwise, they are no longer theories. Theories, presented as theories, remain theories. But if an inference is introduced as irrefutable truth, does it not become a lie? Hence, theories are not to be interfused with our faith. Just as great doubt can be conquered by little faith. Even so, great faith can be defeated by little doubt. This may seem like a meaningless oxymoron at first glance. But if you light a little candle in the corner of a pitch dark room, will the room remain dark as pitch? Of course not. The little candle has defeated the entire room full of darkness. This proverbial candle can represent either doubt or faith. Would you say the Apostle Peter had faith in Christ? After all, he was the first of Jesus' Disciples to receive the Revelation that He was *"the Christ, the Son of the living God"*, (See Matt. 16:16; Mark 8:29; Luke 9:20; John 6:69). But his faith in Christ was greatly shaken by little doubt when Jesus called on him to walk out on the water, (Matt. 14:27-31). Jesus compared faith to a little mustard seed. He explained that if we had faith as miniscule as a mustard seed, nothing would be impossible for us so long as we had no doubt, (Matt. 17:20; 21:21; Mark 11:23-24; Luke 17:6).

The lesson to be learned here is that we shouldn't allow theories to infiltrate our faith. If we combine conjecture with belief our own proud interpretations could react schismatically within the Church.

As it is written:

*"**If any man teach otherwise, and consent not to wholesome words, even the words of our Lord Jesus Christ,** and to the doctrine which is according to godliness; **He is proud, knowing nothing, but doting about questions and strifes of words** whereof cometh envy, strife, railings, evil surmisings, perverse disputings of men of corrupt minds, and destitute of the truth, supposing that gain is godliness: from such withdraw thyself."* (I Tim. 6:3-5)

Again, the Scripture says:

*"Now I beseech you, brethren, **mark them which cause divisions and offenses contrary to the doctrine which ye have learned;** and avoid them. For they that are such serve not our Lord Jesus Christ, but their own belly; **and by good words and fair speeches deceive the hearts of the simple."*** (Rom. 16:17-18)

It is because of these proud interpretations that we have so many unnecessary divisions within the Christian Church. Our Lord said that a kingdom divided against itself cannot stand. Is it the Church? Or is it Churches? Aren't we all members of the same body? (Rom. 12:4-5; I Cor. 1:10-13; 10:17; 12:12-26). One person believes he must be totally submersed to be baptized. Another is satisfied with water poured over the head. What's the difference? Is it the water that does the baptizing? Or is it the Holy Spirit? Is it the head or body that is baptized? Or is it the heart and soul? Paul wrote:

*"There is one body, and one Spirit, even as ye are called in one hope of your calling; **One Lord, one faith, one baptism, One God and Father of all,** who is above all, and through all, and in you all."* (Eph. 4:4-6)

One person believes in celebrating Christmas or Easter. Another esteems all days alike. To the one who celebrates these days, he celebrates them to the Lord. To the one who doesn't celebrate these days, to the Lord he doesn't celebrate them. Some people believe they should eat only certain meats. Others believe they can eat any kind of meat. The ones who do eat give God thanks. The ones who don't eat give God thanks and refrain from eating. What's the problem? Now this would be a whole different story if Christians actually fell down and worshiped the Christmas tree or if they were eating these meats offered to idols. But they don't. We have been made free of all these silly laws, (I Cor. 10:23-32; Col. 2:14-18; I Tim. 4:3-5). The same Christians who criticize the Jews for practicing their ritualistic laws are guilty of doing the same things themselves, (cf. Gal. 4:8-11; 5:1; Col. 2:20-23), thereby reducing the most blessed Sacraments of Christianity into the same kinds of meaningless rituals that circumcision ultimately became to the Children of Israel. But these differences certainly do not need to be an obstacle to spiritual unity. St. Paul wrote:

*"Who art thou that judgest another man's servant? To his own master he standeth or falleth. Yea, he shall be holden up: for God is able to make him stand. One man esteemeth one day above another: another esteemeth every day alike. **Let every man be fully persuaded in his own mind**. He that regardeth the day, regardeth it unto the Lord; and he that regardeth not the day, to the Lord he doth not regard it. He that eateth, eateth to the Lord, for he giveth God thanks; and he that eateth not, to the Lord he eateth not, and giveth God thanks." (Rom. 14:4-6)*

So why are we placing heavy burdens upon ourselves needlessly? If a Christian believes he is free of these things, then he is. And if he doesn't, he isn't. These restrictions could be more disastrous than we think. Consider the following scenario: A certain Christian has bound himself by the old Mosaic Law and believes he should not eat rabbits, (Lev. 11:6). He gets lost in the desert and finds himself at the very threshold of starvation and passes out. When he awakens he finds that a stranger has rescued him. The stranger has prepared a feast of roasted rabbit because it is all he could find in this desolate wilderness and places it before the Christian. Now what is the Christian to do? Will he refrain from eating, embarrass his host, and die of starvation? Or will he condemn himself by eating that which he believes to be unclean? The fact that this Christian is famished has no bearing on the matter. If his faith dictates that he should not eat when his belly is full, it remains in effect even (or more so) when it is empty. Even if the Christian chooses the noblest of his two courses of action and refrains from eating and dies, he has still embarrassed his host, (cf. I Cor. 10:25-27). And if this Christian does eat, he condemns himself because he is not eating through faith. And whatever is not of faith is sin, (Rom. 14:22-23).

These are all trivial matters compared to the rapture and the millennium and the leaders of all denominations should be ashamed of themselves for allowing this to happen, (cf. Matt. 23:23-24). I have much to say about these and other things (eg. transsubstantiation, celibacy of clergymen, whether or not certain individuals should be excluded from celebrating Communion, whether or not the Eucharist should be served with unleavened bread, etc.), but I cannot do so at this time without roaming tangentially from my task at hand.

We shouldn't concern ourselves so much with our own proud interpretations. The only sovereign thing is that God, the Almighty Father, Creator of Heaven and earth, has sent His only begotten Son into the world to be a sacrifice for our sins. He is Jesus Christ; our Lord and Savior; the Paschal Lamb, who bares our iniquities to this day. Moreover, He died on the cross for us and rose from the dead the third day. He is the First Fruits of the Resurrection Power of God; and He lives for evermore. He is seated on the Right Hand of God and will return again to judge the world in power and great glory. He has imparted comfort by way of our Vicegerant, the Holy Ghost. Yea, and more, He has not left us alone upon the earth. For the Holy Spirit of the Lord is with us always, even unto the very end of time. If we pursue righteousness and not evil, we too will join in the resurrection power of the Almighty. We, too, will live with Christ in the mansion He has prepared for us in the Kingdom of God.

We as Christians must follow the example of Christ. He was a King, and yet He became our servant, (Phil. 2:6-8). Therefore, we must be a servant to all, (Mark 9:35; 10:43-44; Luke 17:9-10; John 13:12-16; II Cor. 5:15; Gal. 1:10). We mustn't live for ourselves anymore. We must live for Christ through the Gospel of grace. We must make our bodies a *"living sacrifice"* unto the Lord. As it is written:

"I beseech you therefore, brethren, by the mercies of God, that ye present your bodies a living sacrifice, holy, acceptable unto God,

which is your reasonable service. And be not conformed to this world: but be ye transformed by the renewing of your mind, that ye may prove what is that good, and acceptable, and perfect will of God." (Rom. 12:1-2).

I just want my readers to beware of the many dangers of false doctrine within the Christian community. I want them to realize that it is extremely unwise to believe everything one hears, no matter what credentials the speaker might have or how infallible his argument seems to be. It is far better to be skeptical about what others say regarding the Bible than to believe a fallacy. Believing a lie would eventually lead to destruction and condemnation. When a person follows a lie, both he who follows, as well as the lie, shall fall into the ditch together. But to be skeptical promotes an inquisitive mind An inquisitive mind is able to break any chain of bondage because all limits of learning capabilities have been eradicated. Therefore it is a free mind. And possessing a free mind is one of our most precious tools for understanding the true meanings of the Holy Scriptures.

Every single conception of the Bible must be put to a probative test. Each person must come to his own realization and become completely satisfied in his own mind before making any serious or binding commitments concerning his creed of faith. Search the Holy Scriptures. The answers are there. Anyone who diligently seeks the truth will inevitably find what he's looking for, (Deut. 4:29, James 1:5). The first and foremost step in learning anything is to **want to know**. Anyone who genuinely wants to know truth and prays for wisdom will eventually accomplish their goal. I will close this chapter with the words of Solomon:

*"My son, if thou wilt receive my words, and hide my commandments with thee; so that thou incline thine ear unto wisdom, and apply thine heart to understanding; yea, if thou criest after knowledge, and liftest up thy voice for understanding; if thou seekest her as silver, and searchest for her as for hid treasures; **Then shalt thou understand the fear of the Lord, and find the knowledge of God.** For the Lord giveth wisdom: out of his mouth cometh knowledge and understanding." (Prov. 2:1-6)*

CHAPTER FIVE

THE GOSPELS VS THE RAPTURE

Allow me to provide here a brief summary of some of the things and events I feel could transpire during the tribulation period. My reason for doing so is forthcoming. Throughout this chapter evidence will be produced to substantiate most of my hypothesis. Let me remind my readers that it is just a theory nonetheless. To say I know what the future holds is to claim to be a prophet; and I'm not a prophet. It is preposterous for anyone to make such a foolish supposition, (cf. Num. 12:6). But I don't think it is irresponsible to forward a guess as to the matter. A great deal of my theory is based directly upon Jesus Christ's Own account of the tribulation period, (Matt. 24:1-31). But the first portion of my proposition is highly speculative and is founded upon the prophecies about Gog and Magog in the Book of Ezekiel, specifically chapters 38 and 39. I am merely using this as a "triggering mechanism" to set the stage for Christ's predictions to take place. There are many other possibilities that could trigger the sequence of events depicted in the 24th chapter of the Gospel according to St. Matthew.

AUTHOR'S HYPOTHETICAL TRIBULATION OUTLINE

Russia directs a massive military thrust into the oil rich countries of the Middle East during the winter time. They secure control of the Persian Gulf which brings oil shipments from that region to a halt. The Third World War results. The battle begins with the use of conventional weapons. The Russians realize that the use of nuclear weapons is unnecessary to attain a victory in the Mideast. These nations are relatively defenseless against the mighty Russian army. The possibility of nuclear weapons being dispatched exists nevertheless. Some people might assume this scenario to be unlikely;

especially since the fragmentation of the Soviet Union. But this is precisely why the country is even more unstable than ever before. It's no secret either that Russia's economy is suffering greatly and Middle Eastern oil could be a big incentive for invasion.

The industries and economies of many countries are severely crippled. As a result, gasoline could be strictly rationed. Power plants may begin to decrease output. Electricity may become unavailable in some areas. Water pipes may begin to freeze and fresh water becomes scarce. People may not be able to dispose of waste materials. People residing in such close proximity to one another could prove to be tragic. Due to pestiferous conditions, or possibly terrorist attack, diseases which were thought to be conquered return with devastating impact. Bubonic Plague, dysentery, dyptheria, typhoid fever, malaria, tuberculosis, cholera, smallpox, etc. could spread like wildfire. Food lines and area hospitals may become overcrowded. In many homes heat may not be available at all. Transportation may slow considerably, and in some cases, cease entirely. There might be very little oil and gasoline to fuel trucks, trains, and ships that deliver food to our supermarkets. Children may begin to starve and freeze.

Earthquakes, tornadoes, tidal waves, volcanic eruptions, hurricanes, droughts, floods, extremes in global temperatures, and other cataclysmic phenomena begin to take place with great intensity and frequency worldwide. Consequently, fear and pandemonium abound in the streets.

Now what might happen to those who trusted in the rapture if they weren't taken out of this period of adversity? I honestly don't think many rapture proponents have even asked themselves that question. Most of them are already convinced that they will be exempt from this time of despair. Can we answer that question truthfully? One possible outcome is very conspicuous: Their faith in Christ might totally collapse. Or perhaps they might feel estranged and think Christ had betrayed them. They might feel as though Jesus had failed to keep His promise. Would they realize that this wasn't Christ's promise at all, but the promise of a man instead? At the very least, such a scenario could plant the seeds of doubt in the minds of those who placed their trust in it. I hope my readers are now beginning to understand why I feel this concept to be dangerous and detrimental to Christianity.

Now let's closely examine the account given by Jesus Himself regarding the tribulation period. Here you will see where I derived most of my views in the above tribulation outline. If you've already read any books supporting the pretribulation theory, you may have noticed that they rarely, if ever, quote passages from the Gospels to corroborate their opinion. The reason is because Christ's explanation of the tribulation period directly contradicts the notion of being taken up into the Kingdom of Heaven before it transpires. Jesus declared that His elect, **even His very elect**, must endure this entire period of time before they are taken up (or raptured) into Heaven. Since Christ's predictions lack a pretribulational rapture, proponents of this concept have found it necessary to attach some other complex mode of interpretation to them. Consequently, three predominant theories have surfaced. They are:

(1). Some people are claiming that these predictions, (Matt. 24, Mark 13, Luke 21), have already occurred. They claim that they pertain only to early Christian times and the fall of Jerusalem in 70 A.D. But that idea is unreasonably restrictive for these passages. Since these prophecies concern the end of the world and Jesus' Second Advent, (Matt. 24:3, 29-31), then they cannot, nor should not, be limited to the struggles of Christians around the time of Christ. Has the end of the world or Jesus' Second Coming occurred yet? Indeed not. These things have yet to be fulfilled.

(2). Others are claiming that these prophecies refer only to Christ's gathering of all Jews back to the state of Israel. This idea, too, is irrational. There is absolutely nothing mentioned within these excerpts about gathering Jews to Palestine. These Scriptures speak of Christ's gathering together His *"elect"*, (Gr. *"eklektos"*; Matt. 24:22, 24, 31 & Mark 13:20, 22, 27), and His *"chosen"*, (Gr. *"eklego"*; Mark 13:20). The Greek word *elkektos* rendered as *"elect"* is commonly employed in the New Testament to designate all Christians in general. One example would be:

"Therefore I endure all things for the elect's (eklektos) sake, that they may also obtain the salvation which is in Christ Jesus with eternal glory" (II Tim. 2:10) (Young 164, 293).

For more research on this Greek word and its application in Scripture, examine the following: (*eklektos* translated as "*elect*" = Luke 18:7; Rom. 8:33; Col. 3:12; I Tim. 5:21; Titus 1:1; I Pet. 1:2; II John 1, 13/ *eklektos* translated as "*chosen*" = Matt. 20:16; Luke 23:35; Rom. 16:13; I Pet. 2:4, 9; Rev. 17:14).

The Greek word *eklego* translated as "*chosen*" was sometimes used in the Bible in the same manner. Paul wrote:

"According as he hath chosen (eklego) us in him before the foundation of the world, that we should be holy and without blame before him in love:" (Eph. 1:4)

For more research on the ways this word was employed in the Bible, see: (Luke 6:13; John 6:70; 13:18; 15:16, 19; Acts 1:2, 24; 6:5; I Cor. 1:27, 28; James 2:5).

The Bible says there is no difference between Jews and Christians; both are the children of God, (cf. Rom. 2:28-29; Gal. 5:6). As it is written:

*"**For as many as are led by the Spirit of God, they are the sons of God**. For ye have not received the spirit of bondage again to fear; but ye have received the Spirit of adoption, whereby we cry, Abba, Father. The Spirit itself beareth witness with our spirit, that we are the children of God:" (Rom. 8:14-16).*

Again, another Scripture says:

*"**For there is no difference between the Jew and the Greek**: for the same Lord over all is rich unto all that call upon him." (Rom. 10:12).*

(3). Finally, others are claiming that these predictions are "dual prophecies". In other words, they find their fulfillment at two different periods of time in history. The first would be the Roman invasion of Jerusalem and the other would be the Second Coming of Jesus Christ. This method of interpretation is not utterly illogical and I have no real problem with it. This isn't unprecedented either. Some of the passages in The Old Testament alluding to the coming Messiah are very contemporary and can also be applied to the times of their composition. These prophecies <u>might</u> deal with Jerusalem's destruction: **But <u>they</u> <u>definitely</u> <u>do</u> <u>pertain</u> <u>to</u> <u>the</u> <u>Second</u> <u>Coming</u> <u>of</u> <u>Christ</u>.**

Let's take an in-depth look into the account provided by Jesus concerning the tribulation period and His Second Coming. I will explain these passages methodically; taking them verse by verse. We will begin with the Gospel according to St. Matthew:

(24:3) "And as he sat upon the mount of Olives, the disciples came unto him privately, saying, Tell us, when shall these things be? ***And <u>what</u> <u>shall</u> <u>be</u> <u>the</u> <u>sign</u> <u>of</u> <u>thy</u> <u>coming</u>, <u>and</u> <u>of</u> <u>the</u> <u>end</u> <u>of</u> <u>the</u> <u>world</u>? "***

Then Jesus gave them a step by step list of hardships and afflictions which must transpire before His Second Advent. Furthermore, this question was answered by Jesus with one continuous unbroken chain of events, not two distinct ones. It is obvious that Jesus meant both events (His Second Coming and the end of the world) were consolidated as one. If that were not so, Jesus would've given two separate sets of instructions. He might have said something like:

"My friends, I would not have you to be ignorant concerning my return. Here's what is going to happen at my coming; and then these other events will transpire at the end of time. Let no man deceive you, these are two separate events."

But instead of differentiating between these two events, Jesus gives us only one set of instructions. He certainly didn't say anything like:

"First, I will come invisibly to rapture my church. And then a most dreadful tribulation period will take place. After this period of despair expires, I will come again with My chosen ones to set up a millennial kingdom upon this earth. And after 1,000 years I will destroy this planet."

During the course of our Lord's explanation, there isn't even a hint of a "third coming". **This <u>is</u> <u>one</u> <u>uninterrupted</u> <u>sequence</u> <u>of</u> <u>events</u>.** Here's the discourse given by Jesus in detail:

(24:4-5) "And Jesus answered and said unto them, Take heed that no man deceive you. For many shall come in my name, saying, I am Christ; and shall deceive many."

The very first thing Jesus warns us about is the emergence of false christs. These impostors will mislead multitudes with their claims. Jesus constantly repeats this premonition throughout these prophecies. This is an extremely important aspect of the tribulation period and should be taken very seriously.

(24:6-7) "And ye shall hear of wars and rumors of wars: See that ye be not troubled: For all these things must first come to pass, __but__ __the__ __end__ __is__ __not__ __yet__*. For nation shall rise against nation, and kingdom against kingdom: and there shall be famines, and pestilences, and earthquakes, in divers places."*

Jesus is warning us of some very perilous times indeed. There will be great wars, pervasive hunger, pandemic diseases, and geological calamities occurring worldwide. You might recall I included these conditions in my tribulation outline. Some people claim that these things have been happening for centuries. They have. But it appears that Jesus is suggesting that they will be ingravescent in nature. In other words, they will get worse and worse. It seems Jesus is saying these things will take place with greater frequency and intensity than before. In addition, it appears our Lord is talking about catastrophic battles because He implicitly says they will not cause the end of the world. This is the only time in the history of mankind when a world war could potentially annihilate the entire planet. In the next verse (8), Jesus explains that *"all these are the beginning of sorrows"*. There are still other events to take place before the end comes.

Some religious institutions insist that our Lord is speaking about the end of an age instead of the end of the world here. Basically, that is correct; albeit frivolous. Because, irrespectively, they mean the same thing. For what is the difference between the end of time and the end of the world? Many of these denominations make this distinction in order to verify their conception of a millennial kingdom being established upon this earth at Christ's coming. And this would be impossible if the earth is vaporized at His return. But I will refrain from discussing this idea with any detail for now. I intend to explain these kinds of ideas thoroughly in Chapters 9 and 12.

(24:9-10) "Then shall they deliver you up to be afflicted, and shall kill you: And ye shall be hated of all nations for my name's sake. And then shall many be offended, and shall betray one another."

Thus far our Lord has warned us of false christs, wars, diseases, famine, and geophysical calamities. Now He is saying all believers will be shown antipathy and martyred for His name's sake. Where's the rapture? Surely it would've happened by now! Who is our Lord giving these warnings to? Why would Christ waste His time explaining the tribulation period in such detail if we weren't going to be here when it came to pass?

*(24:11-13) "And many false prophets shall rise, and shall deceive many. And because iniquity shall abound, the love of many shall wax cold. **But he that shall endure unto the end, the same shall be saved.**"*

Only the Christians who endure this period of time "*unto the end*" shall be saved. This clearly shows that Christians will be alive and still remaining upon the earth during this time. They haven't gone anywhere yet. There still hasn't been any hint of a rapture.

(24:14) "And this gospel of the kingdom shall be preached in all the world for a witness unto all nations; and then shall the end come."

It must be noted that the first book ever printed was the Holy Bible. It has been translated in its entirety, or in part, into over a thousand different languages. According to Paul's Epistle to the Colossians, the Bible was well on its way to being proclaimed throughout the entire world even then, (Col. 1:23). I realize the world was much smaller at that time. I'm certain the Gospel will be preached to more and more countries as the time of the end draws nearer. The great tragedy is that in too many cases concepts are being propagated in the Gospel's stead.

(24:15) "When ye therefore shall see the abomination of desolation, spoken by Daniel the prophet, stand in the holy place, (whoso readeth, let him understand)."

This *"abomination of desolation"* is mentioned at Daniel 9:26; 11:31. This takes us into the heart of Daniel's prophecies, many of which are symbolic. This is always a matter of semantics. I'm not very comfortable inserting a lot of inferences into this work. There are numerous opinions and theories about the meanings of Daniel's predictions. I don't know if my opinions would be any more accurate than those of anyone else. It doesn't really matter anyway since they could never be proven. Unless, of course, the Angel of the Lord descended from Heaven and revealed the meanings directly to me. Many people have asserted that this is a reference to the Roman invasion of Judea. This idea is not unfounded. We know from the Bible and history that the Jews still sacrificed animals in our Lord's time, (Mark 14:12; Luke 22:7). It's also a known fact that this invasion ended these practices. This may also have a dual meaning which I discussed earlier. If we compare this reading with the ones we're examining now, there are some noteworthy similarities. Since this deals with the end, (Dan. 11:31), I **think** it might also be a prediction about false christs and the tribulations to befall those who testify against them. I will include the reading here and you can make your own determinations:

*"And arms shall stand on his part, and they shall pollute the sanctuary of strength, and shall take away the daily sacrifice, **and they shall place the abomination that maketh desolate**. And such as do wickedly against the covenant shall he (false christ?) corrupt by flatteries (miracles? cf. Matt. 24:24): and the people that do know their God shall do exploits (giving testimony? Luke 21:13). And they that understand among the people shall instruct many: yet they shall fall by the sword, and by flame, by captivity, and by spoil, many days (martyrdom? Matt. 24:9; Mark 13:12; Luke 21:16). Now when they shall fall, they shall be holpen with a little help (Holy Spirit? Mark 13:11; Luke 21:14-15): but many shall cleave to them with flatteries. And some of them of understanding shall fall, to try them, and to purge, and to make them white, even to the time of the end (end of time? Matt. 24:3, 6, 13, 14; Mark 13:7, 13; Luke 21:9): because it is yet for a time appointed." (Dan. 11:31-35)*

It is not impossible for these readings to find their fulfillment at two different periods of time because we know from Scripture that sometimes history repeats itself:
"The thing that hath been, it is that which shall be; and that which is done is that which shall be done: and there is no new thing under the sun." (Ecc. 1:9) See Ecc. 3:15.
Another aspect that separates Daniel's predictions from those in the Gospels is that the fulfilment for Daniel's prophecies have been calculated (perhaps with a little finagling) right down to the very year of Jerusalem's destruction, (Dan. 9:24-27). But Jesus said that no man, not even He Himself, the Son of God, could know when His prophecies were to take place, (Matt. 24:36; Mark 13:32). It would be downright unthinkable to suggest that Daniel knew more about these things than Jesus Christ Himself. Hence, these prophecies probably depict two totally different events, even though they appear similar in some respects.
(24:16-18) "Then let them which be in Judea flee into the mountains: Let him which is on the housetop not come down to take anything out of his house: Neither let him which is in the field return back to take up his clothes."
Jesus tells the citizens of Israel to seek umbrage in the mountains when they see the tribulation period reach this critical point. I think this may be when the Gentile nations will be ready to attack Israel: (Compare this with Luke 21:20-21). Also, I think this may be reasonable advice for all the inhabitants of the earth to heed. Doubtless, the conditions could be especially severe within the city.
*(24:19-21) "And woe unto them that are with child, and to them that give suck in those days! But pray ye that your flight be not in the winter, neither on the Sabbath day: **For then shall be great tribulation, such as was not since the beginning of the world to this time, no, nor ever shall be.**"*
The tribulation period will be extremely grievous for women with little children or for those who are pregnant. We are also instructed to pray that these things don't occur in the winter time nor on the Sabbath Day. If these trying experiences were to take place at either

one of those times the suffering could be worse than any other tribulations ever exposed to mankind. The ramifications of this statement are mind-boggling and far-reaching. To get an idea of just how bad this could be, compare this with II Kings 6:25-29. I'm almost afraid to print that passage on this paper. It appears that Jesus is saying that there is a possibility of averting this terrible aspect of the tribulation period, if only we pray for it. I suggest we start doing so! I must reiterate here there still has been no mention of a rapture as yet.

Look, I realize these afflictions sound intimidating. I'm not trying to frighten you; I'm attempting to warn you. Listen to the words of St. Paul:

*"Being defamed, we entreat: we are made as the filth of the world, and are the offscouring of all things unto this day. I write not these things to shame you, **but as my beloved sons I warn you**." (I Cor. 4:13-14)*

Should we fear death and adversity or should we fear God? Do you not know that to fear death is to be in bondage to Satan? Do you not know that Jesus came to destroy death and he that had the power of it? As it is written:

*"Forasmuch then as the children are partakers of flesh and blood, he (Christ) also himself likewise took part of the same; that through death he might destroy him that had the power of death, that is, the devil; **and deliver them who through fear of death were all their lifetime subject to bondage**. For verily he took not on him the nature of angels; but he took on him the seed of Abraham." (Heb. 2:14-16)*

Therefore, to fear death is a direct contradiction of our faith in the resurrection of our Lord Jesus Christ. We must be patient when we see these things beginning to take place because our *"redemption draweth nigh,"* (Luke 21:28). All the sorrows and afflictions of this world will be gone for evermore. Of course, tribulation is not desirable. It wasn't meant to be. Otherwise it wouldn't be tribulation. These adversities are nothing compared to the *"eternal weight of glory"* that awaits us in Heaven, (Rom. 8:18; II Cor. 4:16-17). It definitely is a great consolation to know that God would not place a burden upon us which is too much for us to bear. The Scripture says:

*"There hath no temptation taken you but such is common to man: but God is faithful, **who will not suffer you to be tempted above that ye are able**; but will with the temptation also make a way to escape, **that ye may be able to bear it**." (I Cor. 10:13)*

Yes, God certainly knows how to reserve His elect from excessive suffering. But that doesn't mean He will rapture them up into the Kingdom of God. St. Paul said:

*"**And the Lord shall deliver me from every evil work**, and will preserve me unto his heavenly kingdom: To whom be glory for ever and ever." (II Tim. 4:18)*

Was Paul raptured though? Of course not. He was whipped by the Jews five times, forty stripes each time (except once). He was beaten with a rod three times. He was stoned once so severely that he was presumed to be dead. Three times he was involved in a shipwreck. He was robbed and betrayed by his friends. He suffered pain, weariness, hunger, thirst, cold, and nakedness, (II Cor. 11:23-29). According to tradition he eventually suffered execution as well.

Now I'm not saying it is impossible for God to transport a person alive into Heaven. Who am I to say what the Lord God can or cannot do? What about Enoch and Elijah? They were both translated alive into Heaven, (Gen. 5:24; II Kings 2:11). But we must be very careful about making any presumptions here. These were extraordinary events, with extraordinary individuals, under extraordinary circumstances. *"The hand of the Lord was on Elijah," (I Kings 18:46).* Elijah performed exceptional miracles by the Power of God including among other things, bringing a three-and-half-year drought on the earth, raising the widow's son from the dead, and dividing the Jordan River, (I Kings 17:1-II Kings 2:8). Enoch *"walked with God."* One can only try to imagine how righteous he must have been. We also know that God had a secondary purpose for Elijah in preparing the way for Christ in the person of John the Baptist, (Matt. 17:10-11; Mark 9:12-13; Luke 1:17). Whether or not God also had a secondary mission for Enoch cannot be ascertained from Scripture and is not expressly stated.

We must **remember** that these were extremely rare events and **not forget** the words of Christ Himself:

*"I have given them (the Apostles) thy word; and the world hath hated them, because they are not of the world, even as I am not of the world. **I pray not that thou shouldest take them out of the world**, but that thou shouldest keep them from the evil… **Neither pray I for these alone, but for them also which shall believe on me through their word;**" (John 17:14-15, 20)*

It isn't necessary for God to rapture His elect into Heaven to spare them from excessive suffering. How do we know He wouldn't just take their life instead? For what is the difference between rapturing His elect and taking their life? There is no difference. Just because someone is physically dead doesn't mean they are dead to the Lord:

*"Now that the dead are raised, even Moses showed at the bush, when he calleth the Lord the God of Abraham, and the God of Isaac, and the God of Jacob. For he is not a God of the dead, but of the living: **For all live unto him.**" (Luke 20:37-38)*

Let's suppose God decided to spare a certain person from the tribulation period because He decided it would be too much for him to bear. So He takes their life while they sleep peacefully in bed. Wouldn't that spare them of excessive suffering and tribulation? Of course it would. There would be nothing to endure. What better or faster way of meeting death? They would be taken completely unaware. They would feel no pain or fear. And they would be with the Lord. What is the difference between this and the rapture? Listen to the words of Isaiah:

*"**The righteous perisheth**, and no man layeth it to heart: and merciful men are taken away, **none considering that the righteous is taken away from the evil to come**. He shall enter into peace: they shall rest in their beds, each one walking in his uprightness." (Isa. 57:1-2)*

This clearly shows that God can and does spare His chosen ones from evil by taking their life. The real problem is that some people are beginning to fear death more than they fear God. This is how and why such ideas as a pretribulation rapture came into being. But tribulation and death are not to be feared, God is. Death merely hastens a Christian's glorious victory, (cf. I Cor. 15:36). It is far better to die and ascend into Heaven than to enjoy prolonged life and descend into hellfire:

*"And I say unto you my friends, **be not afraid of them that kill the body**, and after that have no more that they can do. But I will forewarn you whom ye shall fear; **Fear him, which after he hath killed hath power to cast into hell**; yea, I say unto you, Fear him."* *(Luke 12:4-5)*

Again it is written:

*"**The fear of the Lord is the beginning of wisdom**: and the knowledge of the Holy is understanding."* *(Prov. 9:10)*

What is death to the Christian anyway? Isn't his physical death in reality his spiritual birth? When a person becomes a Christian he dies in Christ in hope that he may also live with Him in the resurrection:

*"Knowing this, that our old man is crucified with him, that the body of sin might be destroyed, that henceforth we should not serve sin. For he that is dead is freed from sin. **Now if we be dead with Christ, we believe that we shall also live with him**: Knowing that Christ being raised from the dead dieth no more; **Death hath no more dominion over him**. For in that he died, he died unto sin once: but he that liveth, he liveth unto God. Likewise reckon ye also yourselves to be dead indeed unto sin, but alive unto God through Jesus Christ our Lord."* *(Rom. 6:6-11)*

Jesus said:

*"Verily, verily, I say unto you, Except a corn of wheat fall into the ground and die, it abideth alone: **But if it die, it bringeth forth much fruit**."* *(John 12:24)*

And Solomon said:

*"A good name is better than precious ointment; **and the day of death than the day on one's birth**."* *(Ecc. 7:1)*

Were the Disciples afraid of death? No, (cf. II Cor. 5:1-4). In fact Paul longed to die so he could be with our Lord:

*"For to me to live is Christ, **and to die is gain**… For I am in a strait betwixt two (tight spot between two ideas), having a desire to depart, and to be with Christ; which is far better." (Phil. 1:21, 23)*

St. Paul again:

*"**I am crucified with Christ**: nevertheless I live; yet not I, but Christ liveth in me: and the life which I now live in the flesh I live by the faith of the son of God, who loved me, and gave himself for me." (Gal. 2:20)*

Consider this: If there was absolutely no fear of death and/or tribulation within the Christian community, what need or even desire would there be for a pretribulation rapture? If Christians anticipated death as much as they anticipate this rapture, then where would that leave this theory? Would it not become utterly void?

Now let's return to the 24th Chapter of the Gospel according to St. Matthew:

*(24:22) And except those days (of the Tribulation period) should be shortened, there should no flesh be saved: **But for the elect's sake those days shall be shortened**."*

I've heard people refer to this verse as evidence for the pretribulation rapture. That is not the meaning of this passage. This simply shows that God will cut this period of time short for the sake of His chosen ones. This is because if left unmitigated, nobody would survive this trying time. We know from Scripture that there will be survivors upon the earth at Christ's coming, (I Thess. 4:15). Is anything mentioned here in Matthew about ascending into Heaven? No. Why then should we assume that it does?

*(24:23-25) "Then if any man shall say unto you, Lo, here is Christ, or there, **believe it not**. For there shall arise false Christs, and false prophets, **and shall show great signs and wonders**; insomuch that, if it were possible, they shall deceive the very elect. Behold, I have told you before."*

If someone approaches you and declares that he has located Christ, we're not to believe him. These false christs will possess the unusual capacity to perform ineffable miracles in the sight of men; miracles that will be so sensational that *"even the very elect"* would be

81

deceived by them if that were possible.

Now Christ is not talking about cheap tricks, magical stunts, or sleight of hand here. He is talking about downright miracles! The original Greek words for *"signs"* and *"wonders"* in the aforementioned reading are *semeion* and *teras* respectively (Young 887, 1066). These are the same words used in the Bible to describe the miracles performed by Christ and His Disciples. In fact, *semeion* is translated as *"miracle"* and as *"sign"* many times throughout Scripture. One example of this would be:

"This beginning of miracles (semeion) did Jesus in Cana of Galilee, and manifested forth his glory; and his disciples believed on him... Now when he was in Jerusalem at the passover, in the feast day, many believed in his name, when they saw the miracles (semeion) which he did." (John 2:11, 23)

For further references of *semeion* translated as *miracle*, see: (Luke 23:8; John 3:2; 4:54; 6:2, 14, 26; 7:31; 9:16; 10:41; 11:47; 12:8, 37; Acts 4:16, 22; 6:8; 8:6; & 15:12). For *semeion* translated as *"sign"*, see: (Matt. 12:38,39; 16:1,3,4; Mark 8:11,12; 16:17,20; Luke 11:16,29,30; John 2:18; 6:30; 20:30; Acts 8:13; I Cor. 1:22; 14:22; II Cor. 12:12).

Teras was another commonly used term in the Bible to identify the spectacular *"wonders"* of our Lord and his Disciples. One example of this would be:

"And I will show wonders (teras) in heaven above, and signs (semeion) in the earth beneath; blood, and fire, and vapor of smoke:... Ye men of Israel, hear these words; Jesus of Nazareth, a man approved of God among you by miracles and wonders (teras) and signs (semeion), which God did by him in the midst of you, as ye yourselves also know:... And fear came upon every soul: and many wonders (teras) and signs (semeion) were done by the Apostles," (Acts 2:19, 22, 43)

For further references of *teras* translated as *"wonder"*, see: (John 4:48; Acts 4:30; 5:12; 6:8; 7:36; 14:3; 15:12; Rom. 15:19; II Cor. 12:12; & Heb. 2:4).

It is clear that Jesus meant that these Christ impersonators would have the capability to perform genuine miracles. Who has seen a miracle performed? Just think how astounding it would be to witness not only one, but several of them! Permit me to be speculative for a moment.

Millions of Christians have been anxiously awaiting their blessed hope of getting raptured from this period of trial. They have already experienced hardships that were worse than their most frightening nightmares. They are sick, cold, thirsty, hungry, distraught, and perhaps at the very edge of death itself. They might be feeling as though Christ had abandoned them. After all, they were supposed to be exempt from this period of adversity. They are hanging onto their dwindling faith with every ounce of energy they have left.

Then, all of the sudden, a man steps out of the midst of destruction and claims to be Jesus Christ. He explains that it is time to shorten the tribulation period (or initiate the millennium) and that they've suffered enough. He heals mutilated faces, withered bodies, and broken hearts. He heals people who are infected with dreadful diseases and plagues. He miraculously provides food for starving families by converting rocks into bread. He confidently walks down into the polluted waters of our rivers and lakes, inviting us to drink because he has purified them. His philosophy astounds the mind. His powers seem to radiate from his body. Multitudes are following him around to see his astonishing miracles and to listen to his powerful doctrine. Our own relatives, neighbors, and best friends might be standing right next to him, cured and content.

When he walks up to your door, what will you do? Will you stand up and give your testimony against him? You (and I) had better ponder the answer to that before it happens. This is not a prediction of my own: Christ Himself said it would happen. The only hypothetical aspects of the latter are if these impostors perform these specific miracles. But these signs and wonders are only examples of their possible capabilities.

What did you think our Lord meant when He said: *"Behold, I have told you before"*? (Verse 25). He is simply saying: "Hey look, I'm telling you these things in advance so you are not taken aback when they finally come to pass. These false christs will come and will have the competence to perform miracles. So when they arrive, don't allow anyone to convince you to follow after them."

Although these false christs might appear to do only good, they would, in reality, be turning Christians against each other. How could they accomplish such horrendous things? One answer is quite perceptible: What do you think would happen to the individual who walks up to this intruder calling him a false christ in the presence of everyone? Would his followers be overwhelmed with joy when they heard that? The crowd would probably think they were doing a "good deed" for the Lord by executing that person. Listen to the warning of our Lord:

*"These things have I spoken to you that ye should not be offended. They shall put you out of the synagogues: yea, **the time cometh, that whosoever killeth you will think that he doeth God service.** " (John 16:1-2)*

Jesus said that it would be our own relatives and best friends which would be doing these things, (See Matt. 24:9-10, 12; Mark 13:9, 11-12; & Luke 21:12, 16-17). Also, I'm sure these false christs will be well-versed in Scripture and may even attempt to twist the words of Christ around in order to vindicate this action; like His parable of the ten pounds. When the master returned from his journey he found that one of his servants had squandered the money left to his trust. Then the lord of the house said:

*"But those mine enemies, which would not that I should reign over them, bring hither, **and slay them before me.** " (Luke 19:27)*

Oh my God – my God – the power that will be placed in the hands of these false christs! Who will lament, and not rejoice, at their coming? Woe to those of us who profess to be faithful in the Word and are found lacking! Readers, listen very carefully to the words of our Lord Jesus Christ:

*"And shall not God avenge his own elect, which cry day and night unto him, though he bear long with them? I tell you that he will avenge them speedily. **Nevertheless when the Son of man cometh, shall he find faith on the earth?** " (Luke 18:7-8)*

Friends, listen to me: Turn your back on this doctrine and walk away. It is just too risky. If it contains an element of danger, how can it possibly be the truth?

Jesus certainly wouldn't have warned us about these things if we weren't going to be here when they came to pass. Christ said that not *"one jot or tittle"* of the Holy Bible will fail to transpire, (Matt. 5:18). He further stated that man will account for *"every idle word"* which proceeds from his mouth, (Matt. 12:36). He definitely wouldn't go against His own teaching by speaking idle words. And yet, if we were really going to be exempt from this period of distress, that's exactly what He would be doing. Moreover, Jesus said: *"Heaven and earth shall pass away: But my words shall not pass away,"* (Luke 21:33). Why then, would Christ bother explaining the tribulation period in such detail if we weren't going to be here when it happened?

Furthermore, verses 22 and 24 clearly prove that even Jesus' elect would be here on earth during this whole ordeal. They haven't gone anywhere. Some people have suggested that the very elect mentioned here, refer to those who will be left behind after the rapture and convert to Christianity during the tribulation period. Just who will they convert to? The false christs? If Christians *"are the salt of the earth,"* (Matt. 5:13), and that salt be taken from the earth at the rapture, then wherewith shall the earth be salted? If Christians *"are the light of the world,"* (Matt. 5:14), and that light be taken out of the earth at the rapture, then how will people see clearly enough to discern false christs? If these impostors will be able to deceive even the very elect (if that were possible), then just think how easily they will be able to deceive the others. If Christians are raptured up into Heaven before all of this, then just who is going to warn the remaining people of these things? I think we ought to be punctilious about what we are saying. This is no trivial matter. Is it a light thing to meddle with the Holy Word of God?

Honestly now, how many people would turn to Christ during the tribulation period when these false christs are already providing for their every need? How would they even know whether or not these impostors were the real Jesus Christ? Everyone would simply follow these impersonators! What would be the sense in this? A false christ can only do good things for wicked people. These intruders would simply give the people all they wanted.

What these rapture teachers are really saying is that sinners will be given a "second chance" at entering Heaven. Are they not saying, 'Well, if you don't get to heaven in the rapture, you will get another chance to repent during the tribulation period?' But our Lord completely confutes this notion with the following:

"There was a certain rich man, which was clothed in purple and fine linen, and fared sumptuously every day: And there was a certain beggar named Lazarus, which was laid at his gate, full of sores, And desiring to be fed with the crumbs which fell from the rich man's table: moreover the dogs came and licked his sores. And it came to pass, that the beggar died, and was carried by the angels into Abraham's bosom: the rich man also died, and was buried; And in hell he lift up his eyes, being in torments, and seeth Abraham afar off, and Lazarus in his bosom. And he cried and said, Father Abraham, have mercy on me, and send Lazarus, that he may dip the tip of his finger in water, and cool my tongue; for I am tormented in this flame. But Abraham said, Son, remember that thou in thy lifetime receivedst thy good things, and likewise Lazarus evil things: but now he is comforted, and thou art tormented. And beside all this, between us and you there is a great gulf fixed: so that they which would pass from hence to you cannot; neither can they pass to us, that would come from thence. Then he said, I pray thee therefore, father, that thou wouldest send him to my father's house: For I have five brethren; that he may testify unto them, lest they also come into this place of torment. Abraham saith unto him, They have Moses and the prophets; let them hear them. And he said, Nay, father Abraham: but if one went unto them from the dead, they will repent. And he said unto him, If they hear not Moses and the prophets, neither will they be persuaded, though one rose from the dead." (Luke 16:19-31)

This reading sets forth two pertinent ideas: First of all, people will not get a second chance. Secondly, they wouldn't repent even if they were given one.

If Jesus was actually going to rapture His chosen ones before this time of trouble, why not make the last judgment then? Rapture proponents teach that the rapture is totally different than Christ's Second Advent because, at the rapture, He will come invisibly only to take up His Church, but not in judgment. But isn't this rapture a kind of judgment within itself? After all, the only way God could decide who was "worthy" or "righteous enough" to participate in this rapture is to make some sort of judgment.

Are you beginning to see what is happening here? Have you ever heard the old adage, "One lie leads to another?" That's exactly what is happening with this concept. What began as a seemingly harmless fairytale has now grown into one colossal lie. It is contradictory to both Scripture and Christianity.

Now let's get back to the 24th Chapter of Matthew:

*(24:26-28) "Wherefore if they shall say unto you, Behold, he is in the desert; go not forth: Behold, he is in the secret chambers; believe it not. **For as the lightning cometh out of the east, and shineth even unto the west; so shall also the coming of the Son of man be.** For wheresoever the carcass is, there will the eagles be gathered together."*

Our Lord's Second Coming will be so prodigious that everyone will know precisely what is happening. There will not be one single person upon the face of the earth that will not know; dead or alive. Jesus will not reappear upon earth in the form of a human being again (as millennialists claim). He's already done that once. He will appear as a fantastic burst of lightning which will shine over the entire planet. There will be absolutely no doubt in the mind of anyone regarding His authenticity. This includes atheists, agnostics, freethinkers, philosophers, unbelievers, Christians, and anyone else not in that list. But I don't want to venture too deeply into this right now. I will address these things with far greater detail in Chapters Nine and Ten.

*(24:29-31) "**Immediately after the tribulation of those days**, shall the sun be darkened, and the moon shall not give her light, and the*

*stars shall fall from heaven, and the powers of the heavens shall be shaken: And then shall appear the sign of the Son of man in heaven: and then shall all the tribes of the earth mourn, **and they shall see the Son of man coming in the clouds of heaven with power and great glory**. And he shall send his angels with a great sound of a trumpet, **and they shall gather together his elect from the four winds, from one end of heaven to the other**."*

This is the point I've been driving toward ever since I began discussing this particular prophecy. The preceding three verses outright contradict the notion of an upcoming pretribulation rapture. We should not disregard this evidence. Jesus comes to take up His elect **after** the Tribulation period, not before it.

This prophecy would seem to be an insurmountable obstacle for proponents of the rapture. In order to overcome this barrier many people teach that this is only a prediction about Christ gathering Jews to Palestine. I've thoroughly searched out Scripture, but have found no corroborating evidence to warrant these limitations. And, like I said before, others claim that these excerpts pertain only to the early Christian Church era. In this respect, some of these passages may seem somewhat ambiguous. Some of these predictions seem to be fulfilled with the fall of Jerusalem to the Roman army in 70 A.D. But since this prophecy concerns Christ's Second Advent, His gathering of the elect, and the end of time, this method of interpretation is far too restrictive for these passages. See my notes about this on pages 70-71. These kinds of ideas are simply used by rapture advocates to either supplement their own opinions or to disassociate the pretribulation theory from these readings. Don't believe me, read them for your own selves. You don't need a degree in theology to comprehend their meanings. They are not symbolic. Neither are they esoterical. They are transpicuous and completely self-explanatory. If you really want to understand them, then just read them.

All of this was described without gaps, pauses, or intervals. This prophecy is one flowing uninterrupted sequence of events. It isn't until verses 29-31 that anything at all is mentioned concerning Christ gathering His elect unto Him. During this whole discourse on the last times, our Lord never once provides the room for a pretribulation rapture.

Basically, the same account is given for the tribulation period in the Gospel according to St. Mark. The difficulties illustrated in both of these Gospels are virtually identical. Christ's elect must endure the entire tribulation period before getting raptured by our Lord into the Kingdom of God. I will provide the words of this entire reading at length, (Mark 13:5-27). But I will comment only on certain crucial ideas that were omitted in the Gospel of St. Matthew.

(13:5-10) "Take heed lest any man deceive you: For many shall come in my name, saying, I am Christ; and shall deceive many. And when ye shall hear of wars and rumors of wars, be ye not troubled: for such things must needs be; but the end shall not be yet. For nation shall rise against nation, and kingdom against kingdom: and there shall be earthquakes in divers places, and there shall be famines and troubles: these are the beginning of sorrows. But take heed to yourselves: for they shall deliver you up to the councils; and in the synagogues you shall be beaten: and ye shall be brought before rulers and kings for my sake, for a testimony against them. And the gospel must first be published among all nations."

We see here that the Gospel of St. Mark warns us of essentially the same things as the Gospel of Matthew. We've found that He warns of spurious christs, wars, famines, troubles, earthquakes, and our afflictions for His sake. There has been no indication of a rapture as yet.

*(13:11-12) "But when they shall lead you, and deliver you up, take no thought beforehand what ye shall speak, neither do ye premeditate: but whatsoever shall be given you in that hour, that speak ye, **for it is not ye that speak, but the Holy Ghost**. Now the brother shall betray the brother to death, and the father the son; and children shall rise up against their parents, and shall cause them to be put to death."*

When Christians are delivered up to give their testimony, they're not to worry about what to say because the Holy Spirit will put words into their mouths and those words are what they should speak. The Holy Spirit is referred to as *"the Spirit of truth"* often in the Gospel of John, (John 14:15-17; 15:26; 16:12-15). This Spirit of Truth dwells within us, (Rom. 8:9-11; II Cor. 1:22; Eph. 3:17; II Tim. 1:14; I John 4:6; 5:7), and is the most powerful force on the earth today. It cannot be resisted, refuted, or perverted, (Luke 21:13-15). When Christians give their testimony, it will be the truth that speaks, and when the truth speaks, who can resist it? When the Spirit of truth rests upon a person, the effects are overwhelming. Without the strength and grace of the Lord God the presence of the Holy Spirit upon a person's heart would almost be too much for him to bear. The heart and mind of man are very fragile so we need to be instructed very gently:

"Whom shall he teach knowledge? And whom shall he make to understand doctrine? Them that are weaned from the milk, and drawn from the breasts. For precept must be upon precept, precept upon precept; line upon line, line upon line; here a little, and there a little: For with stammering lips and another tongue will he speak to this people." (Isa. 28:9-11)

Besides the return of our Lord Jesus this close protection by the Holy Spirit is definitely a Christian's blessed hope. A true Christian should consider this to be a great privilege, not something to fear, (cf. I John 3:15-16). It is important to bear in mind that when we give our testimony our efforts might give others the courage to come forth and give theirs also, (Phil. 1:14). If someone is truly a Christian, then why would he want to avoid his one chance to prove it? What greater way of displaying one's love for Christ than laying down one's life for Him, (cf. Rom. 16:3)? Jesus said:

"Greater love hath no man than this, that a man lay down his life for his friends." (John 15:13)

What better reason for dying could there possibly be than for the Holy Name of our Lord and Savior Jesus Christ? I realize this may be easier said than done. But unless we continue strengthening and reminding ourselves of these things, our spiritual strength could collapse into pusillanimity just when we need it most. Now I'm not saying rapture believers are recreant. On the contrary, most rapture believers I've encountered are very devout Christians indeed. Why do you think I'm writing this book? Writing this has been a "tribulation period" to me in and of itself. This concept has been a thorn in my side for more than twenty years now. I'm not attacking those who believe in the rapture. I'm attacking the rapture theory itself and those responsible for giving birth to it. So my friends, please forgive me if I sometimes seem to be somewhat acrimonious. Beliefs are delicate matters and it's very difficult to be non-offensive when discussing them. I don't expect those responsible for this concept's popularity to concede error; albeit, I hope they do. But for your own benefit I do expect you to see the error. How can anyone fail to see the big problems associated with this idea?

I would also like to take this opportunity to let my readers know that I am not claiming to have procured a great abundance of the spiritual strength I mentioned. It is unwise for anyone to make the hasty supposition that they are ready to die for the Lord Jesus. This kind of overconfidence and complacency only invites temptation and might put us into the same type of predicament that Peter fell into. He said he would lay down his life for Christ but ended up denying Him three times, (See John 13:36-38). So we should be very careful about such presumptuous claims. All we need to know for now is that it could happen to us one day. If that day comes we must rely on the Holy Spirit for help.

(13:13-27) "And ye shall be hated of all nations for my name's sake: But he that shall endure unto the end, the same shall be saved. But when ye shall see the abomination of desolation spoken of by Daniel the prophet, standing where it ought not, (let him that readeth understand), then let them that be in Judea flee to the mountains: And let him that is on the housetop, neither enter therein, to take anything out of his house: And let him that is in the field not turn back again for to take up his garment. But woe unto them that are with child, and to them that give suck (nursing) in those days! And pray that your flight be not in the winter. For in those days shall be affliction, such as was not from the beginning of the creation which God created unto this time, neither shall be. And except the Lord

*had shortened those days, no flesh should be saved: But for the elect's sake, whom he hath chosen, he hath shortened the days. And then if any man shall say unto you, Lo, here is Christ; or, lo, he is there; believe him not: For false Christs and false prophets shall rise, and shall show great signs and wonders, to seduce, if it were possible, even the elect. But take ye heed: behold, I have foretold you all things. But in those days **after that tribulation**, the sun shall be darkened, and the moon shall not give her light, and the stars of heaven shall fall, and the powers that are in heaven shall be shaken. **And then shall they see the Son of man coming** in the clouds with great power and glory. **And then shall he send his angels, and shall gather together his elect from the four winds,** from the uttermost part of the earth to the uttermost part of heaven."*

Here it is again. My readers must be able to see it! This evidence can not, nor should not be overlooked. Christ returns to gather His elect **after** the tribulation period, not before it.

These predictions of the last times climax with Christ's Second Advent. Once these prophecies reach this climactic point, the question asked by the Apostles was fully answered: *"What shall be the sign of thy coming and of the end of the world?"* At our Lord's return the prophecy is finished. Four times in Matthew, (24:3, 6, 13, 14); twice here in Mark, (13:7,13), and once in Luke, (21:9); these predictions are said to be leading up to the *"end."* Why then, should we assume that Christ's coming to rapture His chosen ones and the end of time occur separately?

Furthermore, the original Greek word for *"end"* in Matthew 24:3 is *sunteleia*, which means "full end" (Young 298). For additional references where this translation is made, see: (Matt. 13:39, 40, 49; 28:20). The Greek word for *"end"* in the remainder of Matthew's prophecy is *telos*, (24:6, 13, 14), which simply means "end". For further references where this translation is made, see: (Mark 13:7, 13; Luke 21:9; 22:37; John 13:1; Rom. 6:21-22; 10:4; I Cor. 1:8; 15:24; II Cor. 1:13; 3:13; 11:15; Phil. 3:19; Heb. 7:3; I Pet. 4:7, 17; Rev. 2:26; 21:6; 22:13). If one researches the above passages and compares the ways in which this word is used, he will see that it is clear that Christ meant His Church would not be raptured until the very end of time and that His elect must endure all these tribulations right up to His coming. As it is written:

"And Moses verily was faithful in all his house, as a servant, for a testimony of those things which were to be spoken after; But Christ as a son over his own house; whose house are we (the Church), if we hold fast the confidence and the rejoicing of the hope firm unto the end (Gr. telos)... But exhort one another daily, while it is called Today; lest any of you be hardened through the deceitfulness of sin. For we are made partakers of Christ, if we hold the beginning of our confidence steadfast unto the end (Gr. telos)." (Heb. 3:5-6, 13-14)

Again the Scripture says:

"For God is not unrighteous to forget your work and labor of love, which ye have showed toward his name, in that ye have ministered to the saints, and do minister. And we desire that every one of you do show the same diligence to the full assurance of hope unto the end (Gr. telos): That ye be not slothful, but followers of them who through faith and patience inherit the promises." (Heb. 6:10-12)

Matthew 24 and Mark 13 should be adequate evidence alone to convince my readers that the pretribulation rapture concept is replete with danger and error. But I'm not finished with the Gospels yet. Now let's take an in-depth look into the Gospel of St. Luke to see if we can uncover any evidential foundations for the rapture. The prophecy of St. Luke regarding the end and our Lord's Second Coming is inexplicably split into two different chapters. Why it is split is unclear and unimportant. It may have something to do with the fact that the Gospel of Luke and the Acts of the Apostles were originally consolidated as two volumes of the same work. They weren't separated and circulated individually until some time around the fall of Jerusalem. Whatever the case may be, they both deal with the same thing. The bulk of Luke's predictions are in the 21st Chapter. Therefore, I will focus my attention on it first. The remaining portion is located in the 17th Chapter. I will address that after I finish with

Chapter 21. To prevent repetitiousness I will refrain from discussing each and every idea, because I've already delineated most of them in detail.

*(21:8-28) "And he (Jesus) said, Take heed that ye be not deceived: for many shall come in my name, saying, I am Christ; and the time draweth near: go ye not therefore after them. But when ye shall hear of wars and commotions, be not terrified: for all these things must first come to pass; but the end is not by and by. Then said he unto them, Nation shall rise against nation, and kingdom against kingdom: And great earthquakes shall be in divers places, and famines, and pestilences; and fearful sights and great signs shall there be from heaven. But before all these, they shall lay their hands on you, and persecute you, delivering you up to the synagogues, and into prisons, being brought before kings and rulers for my name's sake. And it shall turn to you for a testimony. Settle it therefore in your hearts, not to meditate before what ye shall answer: For I will give you a mouth and wisdom, which all your adversaries shall not be able to gainsay nor resist. And ye shall be betrayed both by parents, and brethren, and kinsfolk, and friends; and some of you shall they cause to be put to death. And ye shall be hated of all men for my name's sake. But there shall not a hair of your head perish. In your patience possess ye your souls. And when ye shall see Jerusalem compassed with armies, then know that the desolation thereof is nigh. **Then let them which are in Judea flee (pheugo) to the mountains;** and let them which are in the midst of it depart out; and let not them that are in the countries enter thereinto. For these be the days of vengeance, that all things that are written may be fulfilled. But woe unto them that are with child, and to them that give suck, in those days! For there shall be great distress in the land, and wrath upon this people. And they shall fall by the edge of the sword, and shall be led away captive into all nations: and Jerusalem shall be trodden down of the Gentiles, until the times of the Gentiles be fulfilled. And there shall be signs in the sun, and in the moon, and in the stars; and upon the earth distress of nations, with perplexity; the sea and the waves roaring; Men's hearts failing them for fear, and for looking after*

those things which are coming on the earth: for the powers of heaven shall be shaken. **And then shall they see the Son of man coming in a cloud with power and great glory.** *And when these things begin to come to pass, then look up, for your redemption draweth nigh."*

Here again, we see that the return of our Lord takes place **after** these trying times, not before them. Now let's continue on a little further into this chapter to a passage which is frequently singled out as pertaining to this rapture. Seven verses later we find:

(21:36) "Watch ye therefore, and pray always, that ye may be accounted worthy to **escape** *all these things that shall come to pass, and to stand before the Son of Man."*

Many rapture teachers propound that the word *"escape"* here refers to the pretribulation rapture. But this word should be examined exegetically. This word was translated poorly from the original text and has now become somewhat illusory. Allow me to explain:

In this particular text the original Greek form of the word *"escape"* is *"ekpheugo."* This means to "flee out" or "flee forth". Ekpheugo is translated more correctly in Acts 16:27 and 19:16 as *"fled"*. The prefix (ek) merely denotes which general direction to flee. Other examples would be: (kata)pheugo, which means to "flee down", (dia)pheugo, which means to "flee different ways", and (apo)pheugo, which means to "flee away". The root, pheugo, without a prefix, is translated as *"flee"* in the very Gospel readings we've been discussing, (Matt. 24:16; Mark 13:14; Luke 21:21). These are the passages where Jesus tells the inhabitants of Israel to *"flee into the mountains"* to escape the worst part of the tribulation period. In fact, pheugo is even rendered as *"escape"* twice in Scripture, (Heb. 11:34 & 12:25) (Young 355).

It appears therefore, that Jesus might have meant we could *"escape"* the worst of these troubling times by *"fleeing"* away from them as described earlier. It is important that we abstain from taking this verse out of context and changing its meaning. This reading should not be interpreted figuratively or allegorically. It should be understood in its most literal sense. For example: Escape injury or death by fleeing out of a burning house. As Paul wrote:

"And through a window in a basket was I let down by the wall, and escaped (ekpheugo) his hands." (II Cor. 11:33)

In light of these facts this passage takes on a very different meaning.

Now let's examine the 17th Chapter of The Gospel according to St. Luke. You will see that this reading is inextricably intertwined with the Gospel passages we've already addressed in Matthew and Mark. They undoubtedly depict the same chain of events, but in slightly different words. This is a relatively short prophecy so I will approach it in the same manner as before, taking it verse by verse. I will highlight the various parallels between these Scriptures that prove them to be inseparable. This reading begins at verse 20.

(17:20-21) "And when he (Jesus) was demanded of the Pharisees, when the kingdom of God should come, he answered them and said, The kingdom of God cometh not with observation: Neither shall they say, Lo here! Or, lo there! For, behold, the kingdom of God is within you."

Adam Clarke satisfactorily explains this:

"The Kingdom of God, the glorious religion of the Messiah, does not come in such a way as to be discerned only be sagacious critics, or is only to be seen by those who are scrupulously watching for it; it is not of such a nature as to be confined to one place, so that men might say of it, behold it is only here, or only there: for this Kingdom of God is publicly revealed; and behold it is among you…"

(17:22-23) "And he said unto his Disciples, The days will come, when ye shall desire to see one of the days of the Son of man, and ye shall not see it. And they shall say to you, See here; or, see there: go not after them, nor follow them."

These verses refer to the coming of false christs. Compare this with: Matt. 24:23-36; Mark 13:21; and Luke 21:8.

(17:24-25) "For as the lightning, that lighteneth out of the one part under heaven, shineth unto the other part of heaven: so shall also the Son of man be in his day. But first must he suffer many things, and be rejected of this generation."

This passage is conclusive evidence that Jesus is talking about the selfsame predictions we've already discussed in Matthew about the prodigious nature of the true advent of Jesus. These prophecies are identical and can be compared almost word for word. Our Lord is definitely speaking about His Second Coming here. Compare this with Matt. 24:27.

The next twelve verses are often taken out of context by rapture teachers and utilized to confirm their theories:

*(17:26-37) "**And as it was in the days of Noah**, so shall it be also in the days of the Son of man. They did eat, they drank, they married wives, they were given in marriage, until the day that Noah entered into the ark, and the flood came, and destroyed them all. **Likewise also as it was in the days of Lot**; they did eat, and drank, they bought, they sold, they planted, they builded; But the same day that Lot went out of Sodom it rained fire and brimstone from heaven, and destroyed them all. **Even thus shall it be in the day when the Son of man is revealed**. In that day, he which shall be upon the housetop, and his stuff in his house, let him not come down to take it away: and he that is in the field, let him likewise not return back. Remember Lot's wife. Whosoever shall seek to save his life shall lose it; and whosoever shall lose his life shall preserve it. I tell you, in that night there shall be two men in one bed; the one shall be taken, and the other shall be left. Two women shall be grinding together; the one shall be taken, and the other left. Two men shall be in the field; the one shall be taken (allegedly in the Rapture), and the other left (supposedly to endure the Tribulation period). And they answered and said unto him, Where, Lord? And he said unto them, Wheresoever the body is, thither will the eagles be gathered together."*

The only way this reading could possibly be used to verify the pretribulation theory is take it far out of context and disassociate it with the preceding discourse. There are a few noteworthy aspects of this prophecy which need to be addressed here.

First of all, let's not forget that these verses refer to Christ's Second Coming. The same analogy is made in Matthew following our Lord's discourse there. When using the flood as an example, Jesus said:

"And knew not until the flood came, and took them all away; so

*shall also the coming (parousia) of the Son of man be." (Matt.
24:39)*

The Greek word for "*coming*" in this passage is "*parousia*" (Young
188). And it is a well-known fact that this term always implies the
Second Coming of our Lord, (cf. Matt. 24:3, 27, 37; I Cor. 15:23; I
Thess. 2:19; 3:13; 4:15; 5:23; II Thess. 2:1, 8, 9; James 5:7-8; II Pet.
1:16; 3:4, 12; I John 2:28). When we research these passages we
will see that Christ is definitely speaking of His Second Advent here,
not an invisible pretribulation rapture.

Secondly, many rapture proponents when addressing this passage
have said that since God spared Noah and Lot from doom, it logically
follows that the Church will be spared the tribulation period. But the
Holy Bible denounces such "logical" reasoning:

*"There is a way that seemeth right unto a man, but the end thereof
are the ways of death." (Prov. 16:25)*

These examples of Noah and Lot are not examples of **who** or
how God will **save** anyone. They are examples of God's quickness
in meting out judgment. Just as the flood came suddenly and without
forewarning in Noah's time is just how quickly and without
forewarning Christ will return in His day. And just as quickly and
surely the wicked were destroyed in Sodom and Gomorrah is just as
quickly and surely Christ will pronounce judgment on the wicked at
His Second Coming.

It is clear that Jesus meant that the **times** of these events would
be very similar (*"As in the days of Noah"* etc.), **not the manner in
which anyone is saved**. In the days of Noah and Lot people were
going about their daily business as usual. They were concerned only
with their own affairs and cares of this world. They lacked foresight
and made no provisions for their spiritual lives. Consequently, they
were taken by surprise when destruction came upon them. This was
their own fault. They should have been concerned with their spiritual
lives and not to have left the other undone. This is precisely how the
coming of our Lord will be, (cf. Matt. 24:42-44). We must be alert at
all times and not allow anything in this life to distract us.

Finally, when Jesus says: *"The one shall be taken and the other left,"* He is not talking about an invisible rapture as these rapture advocates claim. After all, verse 30 of this reading says: *"Even thus shall it be in the day when the Son of man is **revealed**."* The original Greek word for *"revealed"* here is *"apokal",* which means "to uncover, unveil, disclose" (Young 814). Every time this word is used in the Bible it denotes a visible event, (cf. Matt. 10:26; 11:25, 27; 16:17; Luke 2:35; 10:21-22; 12:2; John 12:38; Rom. 1:17-18; 8:18; I Cor. 2:10; 3:13; 14:30; Gal. 1:16; 3:23; Eph. 3:5; Phil. 3:15; II Thess. 2:3, 6, 8; I Pet. 1:5, 12; 5:1). The closely related Greek word *"apokalupsis"* (or apocalypse) means essentially the same thing and is frequently used in connection with our Lord's Second Coming: rendered as *"revealed"* at II Thess. 1:7 & I Pet. 4:13, as *"appearing"* at I Pet. 1:7, as *"Revelation"* at I Pet. 1:13, as *"manifestation"* at Rom. 8:19, and as *"coming"* at I Cor. 1:7 (Young 46, 188, 643). Hence, this reading obviously is not the invisible rapture simply because this event does not transpire invisibly. This is an allusion to Christ's judgment when He returns. When Christ comes He will sever the wicked from the just and each will receive their due reward according to their works, (Matt. 13:41-43, 48-50). But I don't want to venture too deeply into this right now. I will explain this with far greater detail in Chapter Nine.

I will now formulate a tribulation outline based upon these Gospel readings:

TRIBULATION PERIOD SUMMARIZED IN 10 EVENTS

• The Tribulation Cycle begins: (Matt. 24:5; Mark 13:5 & Luke 21:8).
• Catastrophic wars, great famines, earthquakes, widespread plagues, and other cataclysmic phenomena begin to take place: (Matt. 24:6-7; Mark 13:7-8; & Luke 21:9-11)
• False prophets and false christs will arise. They will possess the capability to perform fantastic miracles in the sight of men. In so doing, they will deceive numerous people: (Matt. 24:5, 11, 23, 24, 26; Mark 13:6, 21-22; & Luke 21:8)

- The love of many shall wax cold. Friends and relatives will begin to betray one another: (Matt. 24:10, 12; Mark 13:12-13; & Luke 21:16-17)
- Believers will be brought before kings and rulers for the purpose of giving their testimony: (Mark 13:9 & Luke 21:12-13)
- Christians will be tortured and afflicted for the Holy Name of Jesus Christ: (Matt. 24:9; Mark 13:9; & Luke 21:12)
- The Holy Ghost will strengthen and guide Christians during this trying time: (Mark 13:11 & Luke 21:14-15)
- Jesus will "shorten" the tribulation period for the elect's sake: (Matt. 24:22 & Mark 13:20)
- Christ returns as lightning which will shine over the face of the entire earth: (Matt. 24:27 & Luke 17:24)
- Christ appears "in the clouds" after the tribulation period to gather His elect unto Him: (Matt. 24:29-31; 26:64; Mark 13:24-27; 14:62 & Luke 21:27-28)

This concludes Chapter Five of my investigation regarding the Gospels. Remember, Jesus Himself said:

*"I have given them (the Apostles) thy word; and the world hath hated them; because they are not of the world, even as I am not of the world. **I pray not that thou shouldest take them out of the world**, but that thou shouldest keep them from the evil... Neither pray I for these alone, **but for them also which shall believe on me through their word**;" (John 17:14-15, 20)*

Since we haven't uncovered any strong or tangible evidence for a pretribulation rapture within the Gospels, let's proceed to Chapter Six of my inquiry dealing specifically with the Epistles.

CHAPTER SIX

THE EPISTLES VS THE RAPTURE

There are six Biblical passages within the Epistles which are often singled out by rapture teachers as confirmation for the pretribulation theory. Those Scriptures are as follows:

[A] I Thessalonians 4:13-18
[B] II Thessalonians 1:10 & Jude 14
[C] II Thessalonians 2:1-12
[D] I Corinthians 15:50-53
[E] Titus 2:13-14

Although some of these readings do speak of a rapture, or hint at one, they do not state that it will transpire before any sufferings. In fact, not one of these readings even say anything at all about a tribulation period. Since these excerpts do not mention this period of trial, how then, can a pretribulation theory even be fabricated from them? Obviously, this is impossible. Nevertheless, it has been done.

Again, I will explicate these Scriptures individually. I will place each one of them under the microscope and methodically uproot the arguments used by rapture proponents. Also, I realize I am not addressing these passages in the order in which they occur in the Bible. I've done this deliberately. The reason is because the passages in First and Second Thessalonians are, by far, the most commonly quoted among the six.

[A]. I THESSALONIANS 4:13-18

(4:13-14) "But I (Paul) would not have you to be ignorant, brethren, concerning them which are asleep (in death), that ye sorrow

CHRISTOPHER RICCI

not, even as others which have no hope. For if we believe that Jesus died and rose again, even so them also which sleep in Jesus will God bring with him."

These two verses simply say that we shouldn't mourn for those who have died. This is because they are not as hopeless as some people might think. The dead will not be hindered from entering the Kingdom of God just because they have passed away. They still have the opportunity to enter into Heaven when they are resurrected from the grave.

(4:15) "For this we say unto you by the word of the Lord, that we which are alive and remain __unto__ __the__ __coming__ __of__ __the__ __Lord__ shall not prevent them which are asleep."

Those who will be alive and remaining upon the earth at Christ's coming will not prevent them that are dead from entering into God's Kingdom. Certain individuals are claiming that this verse doesn't refer to the Second Advent of our Lord. They say it is Christ's return to rapture His Church before the tribulation period. There's absolutely no evidence here to substantiate such a claim. The tribulation period isn't even mentioned here. These passages ought to be read more carefully.

(4:16) "For the Lord himself shall descend from heaven with a shout, with the voice of __the__ __archangel,__ and __with__ __the__ __trump(et)__ __of__ __God__: and __the__ __dead__ __shall__ __rise__ __first__."

Certain people are saying this archangel represents Jesus Christ. But I'm not so sure that assertion is accurate. This verse seems to make a distinction between *"the Lord himself"* and *"the voice of the archangel."* These appear to be two separate entities. Michael is the archangel of God, *("Yet Michael the archangel..." Jude 9),* and is said to be just *"one of the chief princes"* in the Book of Daniel, (Dan. 10:13). Regardless, this passage signifies the end of this world, the final judgment, and our Lord's Second Coming. Three aspects of this make this an easily proven fact.

(1). The archangel is sent to the world at this time. The only time Michael is sent to this earth is at the very end of time, which is also the judgment day and the resurrection. The prophet Daniel writes:

102

*"And at that time shall Michael (the archangel) stand up, the great prince which standeth for the children of thy people: and there shall be a time of trouble, such as never was since there was a nation to that same time (Tribulation period; Matt. 24:21): and at that time thy people shall be delivered, every one that shall be found written in the book (Last Judgment; Rev. 20:12). And many of them which sleep in the dust of the earth shall awake (Resurrection/ end of the world; I Thess. 4:13-16, John 6:39-54), some to everlasting life, and some to shame and everlasting contempt (Last Judgment; Acts 10:42; II Tim. 4:1; I Pet. 4:5; Rev. 20:12-15)... shut up the words, and seal the book, **even to the time of the end.**" (Dan. 12:1-4)*

(2). Secondly, Jesus comes *"with the trumpet of God"* here. This is a clear indication that St. Paul is speaking of our Lord's Second Advent. This prediction is fulfilled after the tribulation period:

*"**Immediately after the tribulation of those days**... And then shall appear the sign of the Son of man in heaven: and then shall all the tribes of the earth mourn, and they shall see the Son of man coming (Gr. parousia; I Thess. 4:15) in the clouds (Mark 13:26; 14:62; I Thess. 4:17) of heaven with power and great glory. And he shall send his angels **with a great sound of a trumpet** (I Thess. 4:16, I Cor. 15:52), and they shall gather together (Rapture) his elect from the four winds, from one end of heaven to the other."* (Matt. 24:29-31)

Dr. Ironside has asserted that this trumpet here in Matthew is not the same one mentioned in I Thessalonians because the trumpet of Matthew's prophecy is the trumpet of an angel. But, he says, the one mentioned in I Thessalonians is the trumpet of God. Therefore, according to him, these two predictions do not depict the same event. But if one looks closely at Matthew's prophecy he will notice that Jesus sends His angels *"with a great sound of a trumpet."* It doesn't say whose trumpet it is.

I think it is far more than a mere coincidence that **the only time** a trumpet is mentioned in association with the coming of Christ is here in I Thessalonians 4:16, in Matthew24:31, and in I Corinthians 15:52. All three of these passages depict the same event, but in slightly different terms.

(3). Finally, the resurrection takes place at this time. Some people have tried to utilize this to corroborate their rapture theory. They say that the predictions of Matthew, Mark, and Luke have nothing to do with the rapture because a resurrection is not mentioned within them. But they say that since there is one described in I Thessalonians and I Corinthians, then they concern the pretribulation rapture. But just when is the resurrection supposed to take place? Christ Himself said:

"And this is the Father's will which hath sent me, that of all which he hath given me I should lose nothing, but should raise it up again at the last day. And this is the will of him that sent me, that every one which seeth the Son and believeth on him, may have everlasting life: and I will raise him up at the last day... No man can come to me, except the Father which hath sent me draw him: and I will raise him up at the last day... Whoso eateth my flesh, and drinketh my blood, hath eternal life: and I will raise him up at the last day."
(John 6:39, 40, 44, 54)

Again, it is written:

"Jesus saith unto her, Thy brother shall rise again. Martha saith unto him, I know that he shall rise again in the resurrection at the last day." (John 11:23-24)

Jesus Himself says the resurrection will transpire at the end of time. He did not say it would take place seven years before it at the rapture. And those who believe in both the rapture and the millennium are **really saying there are three resurrections.** Are they not saying: "There will be a resurrection at the Rapture, (I Thess. 4:13-16). And there will be another one at the beginning of the Millennium, (Rev. 20:4-5). And there will be yet a third one at the very end of time, (Dan. 12:1-4; John 6:39, 40, 44, 54; Rev. 20:12-15)." We shouldn't be tinkering with the Holy Bible like this. We need to be a lot more careful about what we say regarding the Holy Word of God. But I won't go into this subject right now. I intend to focus on this with far more detail in Chapter Nine. Now back to I Thessalonians:

(4:17-18) "Then we which are alive and remain shall be caught up (Raptured) together with them (the dead) in the clouds, to meet

the Lord in the air: and so shall we ever be with the Lord. Wherefore comfort one another with these words."

Where does it say this event will transpire invisibly? In fact, this is proof that it doesn't. When Jesus comes *"in the clouds"* in Matthew, He emphatically states that we will be able to see Him: *"... and they shall see the Son of man coming in the clouds of heaven with power and great glory"*, (Matt. 24:30). See also Matt. 26:64 & Mark 14:62.

Tim LaHaye in his book entitled, *The Beginning of the End*, has asserted that since some prophecies speak of Christ's return *"as a thief in the night,"* then they concern this invisible rapture. But others speak of it as a discernible event; *"every eye shall see him,"* (Rev. 1:7). Therefore, according to him, they are two separate occurrences. The first represents the pretribulation rapture, and the other Jesus' Second Coming. This is ridiculous. Just exactly what happens when Jesus comes as a thief in the night? Listen to the words of St. Peter:

"But the day of the Lord will come as a thief in the night; in the which the heavens shall pass away with a great noise, and the elements shall melt with fervent heat, the earth also and the works that are therein shall be burned up." (II Pet. 3:10)

Whether these teachers espouse the millennium or not, just to say Christ is returning before the tribulation period is the same as **saying there are three comings of Christ**. Are they not saying: "Christ already came once and was crucified, (John 19:18). He will come again to rapture His church, (I Thess. 4:17). And He will come yet a third time after the tribulation period, (Matt. 24:29-31)". What sort of teaching is this? Of course Jesus came once already. But He is coming only one more time! As it is written:

" For then must he often have suffered since the foundation of the world: But now once in the end of the world hath he appeared to put away sin by the sacrifice of himself. And as it is appointed unto men once to die, but after this the judgment: So Christ was once offered to bear the sins of many; and unto them that look for him shall he appear the second time without sin unto salvation." (Heb. 9:26-28)

I've heard many rapture proponents exclaim: "No, we don't mean to say Christ is coming three times! When Christ comes to rapture

His Church He will return invisibly in the clouds; He will not be seen by everybody." But neither Jesus nor the Apostles ever said He would come invisibly. They did say He would return quickly, (Rev. 22:7, 12, 20), surreptitiously, (Matt. 24:43; Luke 12:39; I Thess. 5:2, 4; II Pet. 3:10; Rev. 3:3; 16:15), and without forewarning, (Matt. 24:44; I Thess. 5:6).

Do you remember when I said: "One lie leads to another?" These teachers have gone to great lengths to corroborate their theories. There is so much embedded error in these concepts that it is difficult to disentangle them enough to refute them. Where do we begin? No judgment day? Two judgment days? Three judgment days? Three resurrections? Three comings of Christ? Invisible rapture? And all for what? To escape physical tribulation, which is a gross misrepresentation and contradiction of Scripture in itself.

Allow me to simplify this text for you: Who is raptured into the Kingdom of Heaven? The resurrected dead and the Christians *"who are alive and remain"* upon the earth, (I Thess. 4:17). Christians who are alive and remaining until when? Until *"the coming of the Lord"*, (I Thess. 4:15). When will Jesus come? He will come *"after"* the tribulation period, (Matt. 24:29; Mark 13:24). How will He Come? He will come *"in the clouds"*, (Matt. 24:30; 26:64; Mark 13:26; 14:62; I Thess. 4:17) *"with the trumpet God"*, (Matt. 24:31; I Cor. 15:52; I Thess. 4:16). What will happen at this time? Christ will *"gather together His elect"* unto Him, (Matt. 24:31; Mark 13:27; I Thess. 4:17). Where will the elect go? They will go up *"in the clouds"*, (Matt. 24:30; Mark 13:26) *"to meet the Lord in the air"*, (I Thess. 4:17). How long will they remain there? They will be forever with the Lord, (I Thess. 4:17). It's that simple.

Verse 18 says we should *"comfort one another with these words"*. That doesn't mean we should twist this excerpt around to possess a meaning that is pleasing to us. Comforting one another is a lot different than creating a false sense of security. We're supposed to comfort one another by explaining that Jesus will raise our loved ones from the dead and He has not left us stranded upon the earth. Instead, He will return again and gather us unto Him just as a hen gathers her chicks under her wings.

It's obvious people must be getting tired of hearing the truth. It seems bland and insipid. But let us hold fast to sound doctrine. For it is written:

"For the time will come when they will not endure (accept) sound doctrine; but after their own lusts __shall they heap to themselves teachers__, having itching ears; and __they shall turn away their ears from the truth, and shall be turned unto fables__." (II Tim. 4:3-4)

Again, the Scripture says:

"As also in all his epistles, speaking in them of these things; __in which are some things hard to be understood__, which they that are unlearned and unstable wrest (twist the meaning around), as they do also in other Scriptures, unto their own destruction." (II Pet. 3:16)

Occasionally some Scriptures are a little abstruse. But instead of carefully scrutinizing these passages to decipher their true meanings, some people *"heap to themselves teachers"* and allow others to do their learning for them, (cf. Heb. 8:11). This is how just a few selected teachers are able to do so much harm. If the teacher is incorrect those who believe what he says could be deceived. There are some people in the world who would do almost anything to obtain a Holy Bible while many of us allow ours to sit in the closet collecting dust.

Some people attend Bible study classes, Bible colleges, Seminaries, etc. I'm certain they initially go there with the right attitude and for the right reason. I agree much can be learned in a good Bible study program. But it is imperative that we make the distinction between truth and theory **at all times**. We must be very careful about letting others teach us about the Word of God. A person does not need another human being to teach him about the Holy Scriptures, (John 6:45; I Cor. 2:12-14; Heb. 8:10-11). The Holy Spirit will teach him in all wisdom and knowledge:

"These things have I written unto you concerning them that seduce you. But the anointing which ye have received of him abideth in you, __and ye need not that any man teach you__: but as the same anointing teacheth you of all things, and is truth, and is no lie, and even as it

hath taught you, ye shall abide in him." (I John 2:26-27).

Now there's nothing wrong with asking for advice as long as it's kept in its proper perspective. But like I said before, if one earnestly searches for the truth, he/she will eventually find it. Sometimes it is helpful to have a good Bible dictionary and concordance. But they certainly are not essential. If a person really wants to know truth and prays for wisdom, he will learn all his heart's desire and then some. Friends, listen to me: It is far better to be a humble Christian than to be a renown college professor with a million theology degrees and miss the simple truth of the Bible. For which is better? To be issued one talent and use it fully and wisely, or to be issued ten, and utilize only nine of them? The Scripture says:

"Better is a poor and wise child than an old and foolish king, who will no more be admonished." (Ecc. 4:13)

And St. Paul said:

"But I fear, lest by any means, as the serpent beguiled Eve through his subtilty, so <u>your minds should be corrupted from the simplicity that is in Christ.</u>" (II Cor. 11:3)

And Jesus said:

"But be ye not called Rabbi (teacher): for one is your Master, even Christ; and all ye are brethren." (Matt. 23:8)

I'm certainly not saying people shouldn't congregate and discuss the Bible. It is good to get involved in programs that promote truth. Jesus said:

"For where two or three are gathered together in my name, there am I in the midst of them." (Matt. 18:20)

Where people gather together in Christ's name He will be present. This can often be felt physically, even by someone who is in doubt. I remember talking about Christ with a Canadian journalist down in one of the cisterns of Masada. We both felt the presence of the Holy Spirit. I know he felt it because he told me so. And before that he wasn't sure if he believed in God or not. But do you think Christ will take it lightly if He sees us entertaining others by declaring conjecture as absolute truth?

Now let's proceed to the next two Scriptural passages on my list:

[B]. II THESSALONIANS 1:10 & JUDE 14

Many rapture teachers say there are two separate comings of our Lord because some Scriptures speak of Christ coming to be glorified *"in"* His saints, (II Thess. 1:10), while others speak of Christ coming to be glorified *"with"* His saints, (I Thess. 3:13; Jude 14). According to them, the first is the rapture, and the second, Christ returning to earth *"with"* His previously raptured Church at His Second Advent. But one merely has to examine these words in their original Greek forms to see that these terms are synonymous and are just different ways of saying the same thing.

In (Jude 14), the Greek word for *"with"* is *"en"*, which means, "in, among, by, with". But in (II Thess. 1:10), the Greek word for *"in"* is also *"en"*. The original words in these two passages are identical and mean exactly the same thing. In (I Thess. 3:13), the Greek word for *"with"* is *"meta"*, which means "with, in common with". Meta is even translated as *"in"* at Mark 14:62 & Acts 15:33. These two Greek words (en and meta) are used interchangeably hundreds of times throughout Scripture. En is translated as *"with"* 139 times, as *"in"* 1,863 times, as *"among'* 114 times, as *"on"* 45 times, and as *"unto"* 9 times. Meta is translated as *"with"* 346 times, as *"in"* 2 times, as *"among"* 5 times, as *"on"* 1 time, and as *"unto"* 1 time (Young 511, 1061). It is obvious that all three of these passages mean the same thing. They do not depict two separate comings of our Lord at all.

The difference in word selection and usage in these passages is just a matter of preference and writing style and is probably due to the fact that there are multiple translators and two separate authors involved. Paul wrote the Epistles to the Thessalonians while Jude, the brother of James, wrote the letter that bears his name. These slight variations in word selection are common occurrences in the Bible because of the many difficulties encountered in translating one language into another. With only a few exceptions the bulk of the New Testament was originally written in Greek, which was the vernacular tongue of the entire region at the time of its composition.

It was first translated into Latin around 150 A.D. But many corrupt translations began to appear and the need for an accurate Latin version was realized. Around 405 A.D. the Vulgate was completed and remained in use throughout the Middle Ages. It was the first book ever printed using the printing press a little over a thousand years later. People first began translating the Vulgate into English as early as the 1300's, but it wasn't until 1611 A.D. that a comprehensive and accurate English version of the entire Bible was completed. This was the King James Version of the Bible. Initially 54 translators were commissioned for this task but only 47 actually participated. These individuals were divided into six groups and the work was carried out at three different locations: two at Westminster, two at Cambridge, and two at Oxford. These three readings might have agreed a lot more if there were fewer translators or if the work had been completed in one location so they could have consulted one another during the process.

[C]. II THESSALONIANS 2:1-12

*(2:1) "Now we beseech you, brethren, by the coming of our Lord Jesus, **and** by our gathering together unto him,"*
Some people have fabricated a pretribulation theory from the word *"and"*! They say that these two events (the return of Christ and our gathering together unto Him) are two distinct events simply because they are divided by the word "and". They say the first event is the Second Coming of our Lord. But, they say, the second portion refers to a pretribulation rapture. However, it is perspicuous within Scripture that Jesus gathers His chosen ones unto Him at His Second Advent, (Matt. 13:41-43; 24:29-31; 25:31-46; Mark 13:24-27), and many others. They are not two separate events simply because they are divided by the word "and". According to this method of interpretation, how could we explain the following excerpt?:
*"Who gave himself for our sins, that he might deliver us from this present evil world, according to the will of God **and** our Father."* *(Gal. 1:4)*

Using the latter mode of interpretation what would this passage mean? Should it mean that God, and our Father, are two separate entities? Of course not.

*(2:2) "That ye be not soon shaken in mind, or be troubled, neither by spirit, nor by word, nor by letter as from us, **as that the day of Christ** is at hand."*

Paul is telling the Thessalonians not to be deceived concerning our Lord's Second Advent. He is letting them know that this event is not to take place for a considerable length of time. In addition, this further shows that the two events depicted in verse one transpire **on the same day**. Otherwise, Paul definitely would have made some type of distinction here.

The *"Day of Christ"* is frequently spoken of within Scripture. Our Lords' return, the rapture (or taking up) of the elect, the resurrection, the last judgment, and the end of the world all occur simultaneously on that day. If my readers wish to examine this further, compare all of the following passages: (Matt. 7:22; 11:22-24; 12:36; 24:36, 50; 25:13; 26:29; Mark 13:32; 14:25; Luke 10:12; 12:46; 17:24, 30, 31; 21:34; John 6:39, 40, 44, 54; 11:24; 12:48; Acts 2:20; 17:31; Rom. 2:5, 16; I Cor. 1:8; II Cor. 1:14; Eph. 4:30; 6:13; Phil. 1:6, 10; 2:16; I Thess. 5:2-4; II Thess. 1:10; II Tim. 1:12, 18; Heb. 10:25; I Pet. 2:12; II Pet. 2:9; 3:7, 10, 12; I John 4:17; Jude 6).

*(2:3-4) "Let no man deceive you by any means: for **that day** shall not come, except there come a falling away first, and that man of sin be revealed, the son of perdition; Who opposeth and exalteth himself above all that is called God, or that is worshiped; so that he as God sitteth in the temple of God, showing himself that he is God."*

Satan is working his way into the Temple of God now. My friends, think about it for a moment. Satan is not out to win the souls of atheists; they're already lost. He is out after the souls of the elect. He wants Christians. Just as our Lord's mission was to save the lost, (Luke 15:1-7; I Tim. 1:15), Satan's mission is to destroy the saved, (cf. II Cor. 2:10-11; 11:3; Eph. 6:10-12; I Thess. 3:5; I Tim. 5:14-15; I Pet. 5:8). The best way for him to do this is to work his way deep into the Church and try to pervert the truth. He wants to work his way into the pulpit. Satan is very industrious and shouldn't be underestimated. He is aware of our weaknesses and will capitalize upon them if we let our guard down, (Eph. 4:27). Satan's ministers are even able to appear as ministers of righteousness. Paul warned the Corinthian Church about this:

*"For such are false apostles, deceitful workers, transforming themselves into the apostles of Christ. And no marvel; for Satan himself is transformed into an angel of light. **Therefore it is no great thing if his ministers also be transformed as the ministers of righteousness**; whose end shall be according to their works." (II Cor. 11:13-15)*

(2:5) "Remember ye not, that, when I was yet with you, I told you these things?"

Obviously Paul had warned the Thessalonians of these things prior to the writing of this letter. He apparently feels these warnings are important enough to be repeated.

(2:6-7) "And now ye know what withholdeth that he (son of perdition) might be revealed in his time. For the mystery of iniquity doth already work: only he who now letteth (prevents) will let (prevent), until he be taken out of the way."

I agree with Adam Clarke's explanation for this excerpt:

"I told you this among other things; I informed you what it was that prevented this man of sin, this son of perdition, from revealing himself fully, **there is a system of corrupt doctrine**, which will lead to the general apostasy, already in existence, but it is a mystery; it is yet hidden; it dare not show itself, because of that which hindereth or withholdeth. But when that which now restraineth shall be taken out of the way, then shall that wicked one be revealed… it will then be manifest who he is, and what he is" (Phillips 566-567).

This may seem a bit provocative and maybe even bold, but I think this "system of corrupt doctrine" is, at least to some degree, antinomianism, the pretribulation rapture, and the millennial theories. Antinomianism deludes Christians into presuming they're predestined for salvation and will escape the day of judgment because abstinence from sin and doing good works are unimportant. The rapture creates the false hope that Christians will be exempt from upcoming tribulation. And the millennium creates the perfect stage for the coronation of false christs.

Many rapture teachers have asserted that it is the Christian Church that is hindering this *"son of perdition"* from being revealed. They say: "He (the Church) must be taken out of the way (or raptured), before this man of sin (antichrist) be revealed."

It must be noted, however, that within the Holy Scriptures, the Church of Christ is **never** mentioned in a masculine gender. Instead it is usually referred to in the neuter gender. But whenever the Church is personified in the Bible, it's **always** done in a feminine gender; **never in a masculine gender**. As a matter of fact, Christ's relationship to His Church is portrayed as a husband's relationship to his wife. Paul said:

*"Wives, submit yourselves unto your husbands, as unto the Lord. For the husband is the head of the wife, **even as Christ is the head of the church**: and he is the saviour of the body. Therefore as the church is subject unto Christ, so let the wives be to their own husbands in every thing. Husbands, love your wives, **even as Christ also loved the church**, and gave himself for it; That he might sanctify and cleanse it with the washing of water by the word, that he might present it to himself a glorious church, not having spot, or wrinkle, or any such thing; but that it should be holy and without blemish... This is a great mystery: **But I speak concerning Christ and the church**."* (Eph. 5:22-32)

Again, the Scripture says:

*"For I (Paul) am jealous over you (the Church) with godly jealousy: for I have espoused you to one husband, that I may present you as a **chaste virgin** to Christ."* (II Cor. 11:2)

The Church is illustrated in the Book of Revelation as a bride adorned for her husband which is Jesus Christ:

*"Let us be glad and rejoice, and give honor to him (Christ): for the marriage of the Lamb is come, and **his wife** (the Church) hath made **herself** ready. And to **her** was granted that **she** should be arrayed in fine linen, clean and white: for the fine linen is the*

righteousness of the saints. And he saith unto me, Write, Blessed are they which are called unto the marriage supper of the Lamb. And he saith unto me, These are the true sayings of God." (Rev. 19:6-9). See also Rev. 22:17.

Christ's relationship to the Church is a carryover of ancient Jewish tradition. In the Old Testament, God's love for and covenant with Israel is described in terms of a marriage relationship as well, (cf. Isa. 1:21; 62:5; Jer. 3:1; Eze. 16 & 23; Hosea 1-3). Now I'm not certain just what it is which is preventing this son of perdition from being revealed. But I am certain it is not the Church.

*(2:8-12) "And then shall that Wicked be revealed, whom the Lord shall consume with the spirit of his mouth, and shall destroy with the brightness of his coming: Even him, whose coming is after the working of Satan with all power and signs and lying **wonders**, and with all deceivableness of unrighteousness in them that perish; **because they received not the love of the truth**, that they might be saved. **And for this cause God shall send them strong delusion, that they should believe a lie.** That they all might be damned who believed not the truth, but had pleasure in unrighteousness."*

This "man of sin" will possess the unusual capability to perform sensational miracles. The original Greek word for *"wonders"* here is *"teras"*. This is the same word used in the Bible to describe the miracles that Christ performed. See the references provided on pages 81-83. It appears Paul is speaking about false christs here, (cf Matt. 24:24; Mark 13:22). Many people claim this is a reference to the antichrist of the Revelation represented by the number 666. But they are only guessing as to the matter. I will discuss these kinds of ideas with far more detail in Chapters Ten and Eleven. Whoever or whatever Paul is referring to, it will be destroyed by the brightness of Christ's return. The only reason this *"son of perdition"* will be so powerful and influential is because his followers will stray from the truth. And because of this, *"God shall send them strong delusion that they should believe a lie"*. See my notes on false doctrine and the wrath of God in Chapter Four.

As my readers may have noticed, I deliberately did not put the last sentence of this passage in bold print as I was very much inclined to do. I want my readers to know that I am very worried about this concept's impact on Christianity. I personally know many good Christians who believe wholeheartedly in this over-exaggerated concept. I need for them to understand that it is not too late to walk away from this theory. It's fine to hope to escape physical suffering; I'd like to escape it too. But if I live to see it, I don't think I am going to escape anything. Don't you think I've searched for a way out myself? I place my hope and trust in the Lord God Almighty and no matter what His will may be, let it be done to His glorification. When I initially heard of this rapture I believed it as well. After all, the individuals who were advancing the idea were far more educated than I was. And since so many other people believed it too, it went without saying that it must have been the truth. It wasn't until I began to search the Bible for evidence of it that I began to feel something was very much amiss. I searched high and low for Scriptural support for it but I couldn't find any strong evidence for it anywhere in the Bible. This really concerned me and that's when I embarked on this mission of writing a book about it. If you ask the Holy Spirit to help you with this, the Spirit of Truth, I'm confident He will. What do you have to lose?

[D]. I CORINTHIANS 15:50-53

*"Now this I say, brethren, that flesh and blood cannot inherit the kingdom of God; neither doth corruption inherit incorruption. Behold, I show you a mystery; we shall all not sleep (die), but we shall all be changed, in a moment, in the twinkling of an eye, **at the last trump(et), For the trumpet shall sound** (Second Coming, Matt. 24:31; I Thess. 4:16), **and the dead shall be raised incorruptible** (Resurrection, John 6:39, 40, 44, 54), and we shall be changed. For this corruptible must put on incorruption, and this mortal must put on immortality."*

There is a hint of a rapture here. But where's the tribulation period? There's absolutely no indication here that a rapture occurs before

115

any time of trouble. There isn't even anything at all mentioned here about the tribulation period. How then can a pretribulation theory even be constructed from this? I find it hard to believe that it has even been done! How can my readers fail to see what I'm talking about? I don't understand how this has gone unchecked for so long.

Many individuals are claiming that this *"mystery"* is the rapture. The real mystery is how they've arrived at such a far gone conclusion. This mystery certainly is not the pretribulation rapture. It is the fact that we all shall not die as must have been presupposed by the Corinthians at that time. This mystery is the fact that *"we which are alive and remain unto the coming of the Lord"* shall be caught up into Heaven and our bodies will be changed from mortal to immortal. This apparently was a new idea to the Corinthians at the time. This passage says basically the same things as I Thess. 4:13-18.

This reading indicates our Lord's Second Coming and the end of time. The sounding of the "last trumpet" and the fact that the resurrection occurs at this time is sufficient evidence to prove that. See my observations on pages 102-104.

Mr Phillips simplifies this text quite well when he writes:

"Listen, and I shall tell you a secret. We shall not all die, but suddenly, in the twinkling of an eye, every one of us will be changed as the trumpet sounds! The trumpet will sound and the dead shall be raised beyond the reach of corruption, and we who are still alive shall suddenly be utterly changed. For this perishable nature of ours must be wrapped in imperishability; these bodies which are mortal must be wrapped in immortality. So when the perishable is lost in the imperishable, the mortal lost in the immortal, this saying will come true: Death is swallowed up in victory."

[E]. TITUS 2:13-14

*"Looking for that **blessed hope**, and the glorious **appearing** of the great God and our Saviour Jesus Christ; Who gave himself for us, that he might redeem us from all iniquity, and purify unto himself a peculiar people, zealous of good works."*

This excerpt too, says absolutely nothing about a pretribulation rapture. Many rapture teachers claim that this "blessed hope" is the rapture. By doing so they convert that hope into a false hope. This blessed hope is the glorious reappearing of our Lord Jesus Christ, who died for us so that we might obtain redemption of sins. That is all this passage means, nothing more, nothing less.

Moreover, the original Greek word for *"appearing"* in this text is *"epiphaneia"* which means "manifestation" (Young 46, 116). And we've already discussed the fact that this rapture is supposed to transpire invisibly. Epiphaneia is rendered as *"appearing"* four other times in Scripture, (I Tim. 6:14; II Tim. 1:10; 4:1, 8), and as *"brightness"* once, (II Thess. 2:8). Every time this word is employed in the Bible it denotes the very visible Second Coming of our Lord. This should be used to contradict the rapture, not as evidence to bolster it.

CHAPTER SEVEN

CLOSING NOTES ON THE RAPTURE THEORY.

Can you see why the rapture is such a threatening concept now? The most dangerous aspect of it has to be that it procreates false hope. What could possibly be worse than false hope? By saying this rapture occurs before this period of distress these people are really saying, "peace, peace," when there is no peace. Are they not saying?:

"Be of good cheer; be at peace my friends! For if you truly believe in Christ and maintain a good Christian lifestyle, you will not have to suffer any of the afflictions which are about to befall mankind in the tribulation period. The Lord Jesus will extract all His chosen ones from the earth before it comes to pass. So don't be concerned because Christ considers you worthy to be exempt from this period of trial."

But Paul said:

*"For yourselves know perfectly that the day of the Lord so cometh as a thief in the night. **For when they shall say, peace and safety; then sudden destruction cometh upon them**, as travail upon a woman with child; **and they shall not escape**." (I Thess. 5:2-3)*

Ezekiel warned the prophets of Israel about this very thing over 2,500 years ago:

*"Son of man, prophesy against the prophets of Israel that prophesy, and say thou unto them that prophesy out of their own hearts, Hear ye the word of the Lord; Thus saith the Lord God; Woe unto the foolish prophets, that follow their own spirit, and have seen nothing! O Israel, thy prophets are like the foxes in the deserts. Ye have not gone up into the gaps, **neither made up the hedge for the house of Israel to stand in the battle in the day of the Lord**. They have seen vanity and lying divination, saying, the Lord saith: and the Lord hath not sent them: and they have made others to hope that they would confirm the word. Have ye not seen a vain vision, and*

*have ye not spoken a lying divination, whereas ye say, The Lord saith it; albeit I have not spoken? Therefore thus saith the Lord God; Because ye have spoken vanity, and seen lies, therefore, behold, I am against you, saith the Lord God. And mine hand shall be upon the prophets that see vanity, and that devine lies: they shall not be in the assembly of my people, neither shall they be written in the writing of the house of Israel, neither shall they enter into the land of Israel; and ye shall know that I am the Lord God. Because, **even because they have seduced my people, saying, peace, and there was no peace**; and one built up a wall; and, lo, others daubed it with untempered mortar: Say unto them which daubed it with untempered mortar, **that it shall fall**: there shall be an overflowing shower; and ye, O great hailstones, shall fall; and a stormy wind shall rend it. Lo, when the wall is fallen, shall it not be said unto you, **Where is the daubing wherewith ye have daubed it?** (Eze. 13.2-12)* See also Jer. 8:10-15 and 23:15-22).

How relevant this saying is! These individuals have built a protective wall around Christians that doesn't belong there. And when it comes crumbling down, will they not say: *"Where is the daubing wherewith ye have daubed it?"* I've debated long and hard on whether or not I should include these sayings because of their severity. But I cannot spare them. Are they not the truth?

I've heard so many ministers, evangelists, and Biblical scholars harp on and on about how many people have turned to and believed in Christ after hearing of this merciful rapture. But have they ever considered the devastating consequences that could result if it didn't take place? Did they ever consider how many people might turn away from or disbelieve in Christ if this rapture fails to occur before these trying times? Friends, I beg of you: Alert your followers to these possible dangers. This theory cannot be looked at unilaterally anymore. If this rapture doesn't take place as proposed, how will you be able to bear the burdens of responsibility and improvidence? A time of great confusion for the Christian community is fast approaching. Friends, listen to me: Don't turn a deaf ear to what I'm saying. Ponder it within your hearts. Can anyone honestly say that I speak a lie?

In April of 1986, I traveled around the United States to circulate an earlier version of this book. One of my stops was The Jimmy Swaggart Bible College in Baton Rouge, LA. I was accepted and listened to and I am grateful. The members of this particular establishment generally support the pretribulation rapture theory. Shortly thereafter, I received a small pamphlet in the mail about the rapture entitled, *Will the Church go through The Great Tribulation period?* Inside, Mr. Swaggart, in effect, concedes that there may be an element of risk associated with the rapture concept. In the pamphlet he states that in recent years there has been mounting opposition to the rapture theory. He says opponents of this idea are beginning to warn Christians with the following logic: If Christians prepare themselves to endure the tribulation period and are spared, they lose nothing and gain everything. But if Christians who count on this rapture don't prepare themselves for this period of adversity and are not spared, they stand to lose it all. Mr. Swaggart goes on to explain that although this may be a logical standpoint, proponents of this view must be seeking punishment.

There are a number of important observations to be noted here. First of all, it is not opposition to this view that has surfaced recently; it is adherence to it. A hundred years ago this idea was basically nonexistent. The number of naïve Christians embracing the rapture concept is growing exponentially; especially since the recent release of Tim LaHaye's *Left Behind* series. This idea is being advanced all around the globe in alarming speed. This has got to be stopped.

Secondly, if there is a logical argument against this concept, then it is not worthy of wholehearted belief. Many individuals consider this theory as irrefutable truth. I know because I've talked with many of them personally. Logical arguments cannot be constructed against truth. Otherwise, they are illogical arguments. Logical arguments can only be constructed against concepts, views, theories, or opinions. Truth is truth. It is indefeasible. It cannot change. It cannot be altered. Neither can it be refuted. It will remain truth forever. But concepts are defeasible. Views can change. Theories can be altered. And opinions can be refuted. If there is a logical argument against a given viewpoint, imperfection and uncertainty are present and it has no place with irrefutable truth. If there **is any chance whatsoever** of the rapture failing to take place before the tribulation period then it is not worthy of unwavering acceptation. It's that simple.

Finally, I wouldn't say that Christians who prepare to endure the tribulation period are seeking punishment. I'd say they are seeking the truth. If the truth is that we are to be here when this period of trial happens, then we need to gird up our loins and face it with faith and patience. I'd say that we all should expect correction and tribulation but hope for God's mercy. For it is a fact that all have sinned and have fallen short of the glory of the Lord, (Luke 13:1-5; 17:9-10; Rom. 3:23). And even the righteousness of the most righteous individuals is as *"filthy rags"*, (Isa. 64:6). It is only by the grace of God that we have any opportunity to enter the Kingdom of God, (Eph. 2:8-9). This undoubtedly is the most rational standpoint. Like the age-old aphorism: "Prepare for the worst but hope for the best." This way we cannot be disappointed.

There are **hundreds of thousands** of people with various religious backgrounds who believe wholeheartedly in this farfetched concept. Any preacher, pastor, theologian, evangelist, or common Christian who disagrees with this idea and allows it to continue is adding onto the problem. Some people might say: "Let them believe what they want to believe." What kind of a Christian is that? These are your beloved brothers and sisters! I thank God the Disciples didn't think that way. Perhaps these people don't realize that failing to speak out in dissension regarding this issue is the same as being acquiescent? Closing one's eyes to the truth makes him just as guilty as the perpetrator, (Lev. 20:4-5). Perhaps some of these people simply did not realize the austerity of this matter? Or, perhaps these people are underestimating the problem? Perhaps some of these people might think that since they don't embrace or advance this theory themselves, then they are free from all responsibility? That type of logic could be compared appropriately to the Holocaust of World War II.

Six million Jews were systematically slaughtered by the Nazis in three years. Who was responsible for this disgrace? Does the blame rest solely on the Third Reich? Or should some of the blame be placed on all the government leaders who knew it was happening and did nothing to stop it? Six million people don't just vanish from the face of the earth without someone knowing about it. It is a fact that other government leaders were cognizant of it. However, they underestimated the problem. Therefore, nations such as the United States chose to remain neutral in the war. It wasn't until the bombing of Pearl Harbor that the U.S. finally was forced to emerge from its shell.

Permit me to expound this "parable" and its relation to the rapture concept: The Nazis represent the teachers of this rapture theory. The Jews represent the innocent Christians that are misled by that concept. The neutral nations represent the religious leaders that choose to remain indifferent and ignore the problem. The bombing of Pearl Harbor represents Jesus' Second Advent and the judgment.

The rapture concept is damaging the faith of hundreds of thousands of Christians. Meanwhile, our religious leaders allow this to take place and remain reticent. And when Christ comes who do you think will be held responsible for the damage done? Pretending to be ignorant of the problem is the same as creating it:

"If thou faint in the day of adversity, thy strength is small. If thou forbear to deliver them that are drawn unto death, and those that are ready to be slain; if thou sayest, Behold, we knew it not; doth not he that pondereth the heart consider it? And he that keepeth thy soul, doth not he know it? And shall not he render to every man according to his works?" (Prov. 24:10-12)

Again it is written:

"If there come any unto you, and bring not this doctrine, receive him not into your house, neither bid him Godspeed: For he that biddeth him Godspeed is partaker of his evil deeds." (II John 10-11)

I realize these may seem like severe comparisons. But they do convey my message well. This is a serious problem and it calls for rigorous solutions.

I've noticed a very curious phenomenon with this rapture. It seems the teachers advancing this idea have convinced their followers that to doubt this concept's integrity is to jeopardize their chances of participating in it. This idea has been put on a pedastal equal with

God Almighty! It seems like these teachers are saying that to doubt this concept is the same as wavering in our faith in Christ or the Lord God. This is complete and utter nonsense. The Bible says we should *"try the spirits whether they are of God: because many false prophets are gone out into the world."* (I John 4:1) To be skeptical about this idea does not in any way minimize one's chances of partaking in it. If anything, it would maximize them. Wasn't Gideon skeptical when the Spirit of the Lord appeared to him? He boldly tested the Angel of the Lord three times without kindling the wrath of God, (Judges 6:17, 36-40). If God wasn't angry with Gideon for doubting His own angel why should we worry about doubting a man-made idea? God **expects** us to do this.

I know my readers will examine this inquisition with some degree of skepticism. I absolutely respect that. But before you cast this book aside and outright reject it, let me advise you of this: If there's any possibility that I'm correct about this theory, then hadn't you better contemplate it? It is every Christian's duty to weigh the facts on religious issues and draw a reasonable conclusion as to the matter. Either my readers determine that I don't know what I'm talking about, or they conclude that this examination does possess merit and is worthy of serious consideration.

If one decides this book is meritorious in any way, then he must concur that the rapture is a conception of man and not a precept of Christ. That is basically all I intended to prove. It is not necessary for me to prove the rapture concept to be consummately erroneous; albeit, I think I have. It is only necessary for me to prove that it is merely an invention contrived in the mind of a man. If the rapture is a theory in any sense of the word, then it is unworthy of wholehearted belief. One should only believe in that which he has absolutely no doubt about. If an individual questions the integrity of this conception and still continues to believe it, then he is fooling his own self. To fool one's self is totally hypocritical and contradictory. He is both the fooler and the fool. The greatest fool is he who has somehow managed to fool himself. If we take all the arguments both for and against this idea, throw them into a large kettle and boil it down, what are we left with at the bottom of the pot? Doubt and uncertainty. Can you still say you believe in this rapture as much as you believe in God, Christ, or the Holy Spirit? If you can't say that, this rapture is unworthy of unfaltering belief.

Many Christians believe in this idea because of the incessant preaching on the subject and/or lack of preaching against it. Now a drastic situation has resulted. It doesn't seem to matter how much evidence I produce portraying the dangers associated with this idea. Many people will continue to believe it nonetheless. This concept has been "pounded" into the minds and hearts of these Christians and now they've become pertinacious and totally indoctrinated. They refuse to change their minds on the matter. They've been told not to listen to anyone else because they risk being deceived. But unbeknownst to them they've already been deceived. Now their beliefs have become virtually irreversible.

All I ask of my readers is to weigh the facts. The Scriptural facts I've advanced against this idea outweigh the arguments supporting it overwhelmingly. So much so, they demand consideration. I think my readers will be able to see that. At the very least my readers will be better prepared if this rapture fails to take place as proposed. I will close this chapter with this exhortation:

*"Wherefore take unto you the whole armor of God, **that ye may be able to withstand in the evil day**, and having done all, to stand. Stand therefore, having your loins girt about with truth, and having on the breastplate of righteousness, and your feet shod with the preparation of the Gospel of peace; above all, taking the shield of faith, wherewith ye shall be able to quench all the fiery darts of the wicked. And take the helmet of salvation, and the sword of the Spirit, which is the word of God: Praying always with all perseverance and supplication for all saints." (Eph. 6:13-18)*

Friends and neighbors: Hang in there. Exercise tolerance, vigilance, temperance, and benevolence. And may God the Father of our Lord and Savior Jesus Christ bless and keep you all.

CHAPTER EIGHT

THE MILLENNIUM

First of all, allow me to redefine the word "millennium". Again, this particular word is not to be found within the Holy Bible. It is a Latin word designating the thousand-year theocracy described in the twentieth chapter of the Book of Revelation. I will include the entire reading here for the benefit of my readers: (Rev. 20:1-15). This way you won't have to keep reverting back to your Bible to find it.

*"[1] And I saw an angel come down from heaven, having the key of the bottomless pit and a great chain in his hand. [2]. And he laid hold on the dragon, that old serpent, which is the Devil, and Satan, and bound him a thousand years, [3]. And cast him into the bottomless pit, and shut him up, and set a seal upon him, that he should deceive the nations no more, till the thousand years should be fulfilled: and after that he must be loosed a little season. [4]. And I saw thrones, and they sat upon them, and judgment was given unto them: and I saw the souls of them that were beheaded for the witness of Jesus, and for the word of God, and which had not worshiped the beast, neither his image, neither had received his mark upon their foreheads, or in their hands; **and they lived and reigned with Christ a thousand years** (the Millennium). [5]. But the rest of the dead lived not again until the thousand years were finished. This is the first resurrection. [6]. Blessed and holy is he that hath part in the first resurrection: on such the second death hath no power, but they shall be priests of God and of Christ, and shall reign with him a thousand years. [7]. And when the thousand years are expired, Satan shall be loosed out of his prison, [8]. And shall go out to deceive the nations which are in the four quarters of the earth, Gog and Magog, to gather them together to battle: the number of whom is as the sand of the sea. [9]. And they went up on the breadth of the earth, and compassed the camp of the saints about, and the beloved city: and*

*fire came down from God out of heaven, and devoured them. [10].
And the Devil that deceived them was cast into the lake of fire and
brimstone, where the beast and the false prophet are, and shall be
tormented day and night for ever and ever. [11]. And I saw a great
white throne, and him that sat on it, from whose face the earth and
the heaven fled away; and there was found no place for them. [12].
And I saw the dead, small and great, stand before God; and the
books were opened: and another book was opened, which is the book
of life: and the dead were judged out of those things which were
written in the books, according to their works. [13]. And the sea
gave up the dead which were in it; and death and hell delivered up
the dead which were in them: and they were judged every man
according to their works. [14]. And death and hell were cast into the
lake of fire. This is the second death. [15]. And whoever was not
found written in the book of life was cast into the lake of fire."*

Many people are saying that there will be a thousand years of
peace and tranquility upon this earth. In addition, they are claiming
that Jesus Christ Himself will come down upon the earth to launch
this hagiocracy; or government by saints.

If my readers have a different conception of the millennium than
the latter, this is not a critique of your beliefs. As long as the idea of
Christ reappearing upon this planet is omitted, I see no harm in any
other interpretation. But in many cases people declare that Jesus
will initiate the millennium personally. That idea is dangerous with
respect to the coming of false christs.

The millennial conception is much older that the rapture concept.
In fact, I've failed to fix a definite date for the introduction of the
pretribulation rapture concept. But it is much younger than the
millennium comparatively. The millennium, therefore, is far more
embedded into Christian thought. Its roots can be traced deep into
the early Christian Church age; probably even as far back as the
writing of the Revelation around the fall of Jerusalem in 70 A.D.
The actual date for the writing of the apocalypse is questionable, so
I'm not going to engage in this unimportant debate. The millennium
has had varying degrees of popularity and acceptance over the

centuries. It seems that when times were prosperous its popularity faded correspondingly. And when world events appeared portentous its popularity would once again rebound. But now after two World Wars and the invention of the hydrogen bomb, coupled with Christ's ominous predictions of a tribulation period, hopes and expectations for an upcoming millennium have risen dramatically. These things have brought the millennium to the forefront of Christian eschatology as never before. Now I've found myself in a quagmire of fallacious arguments about this idea. Hence, I will need to divide this section into five chapters to maintain a continuous and congruous investigation. I'll delineate those divisions now so my readers can see my train of thought and get a basic idea of where I'm going with this:

• Chapter Nine: Jesus' Second Coming, the assumption, the last judgment, the end of the world, and the resurrection are all one and the same event. There is not a thousand-year period between any two of those events.

• Chapter Ten: The risk of false christs associated with the millennial concept.

• Chapter Eleven: The danger of meddling with the message or meanings of the Book of Revelation.

• Chapter Twelve: The "Everlasting Kingdoms". These kingdoms do not concern the millennium because it doesn't last forever. Also, this earth will not endure forever. Hence, these kingdoms will not occur upon this earth.

• Chapter Thirteen: The battle with Gog and Magog following the millennium. If these entities are identical with those of the same name in the Book of Ezekiel, the theories of many chiliasts (millennialists) will be called into question.

CHAPTER NINE

JESUS' SECOND ADVENT VS THE MILLENNIUM

When Christ comes He is not going to bring in a thousand years of peace and harmony to this earth. Instead, He will judge between the righteous and the wicked at that time. He is not going to "put judgment off" for a thousand years. When Jesus returns all nations and peoples will be gathered before Him. Christ will sit upon the throne of judgment. Then He will judge every man according to his own deeds. This is the final judgment; the righteous people shall ascend into the Kingdom of Heaven and the wicked people shall descend into hellfire. Jesus said:

"__When the Son of man shall come in his glory__, and all the holy angels with him (Second Coming: Matt. 16:27; 24:30-31; Mark 8:38; 13:26-27), __Then shall he sit upon the throne of his glory__: And before him shall be gathered all nations: And he shall separate them one from another, as a shepherd divideth his sheep from his goats (Last Judgment: Matt. 13:49-50): Then shall the King say unto them on his right hand, come, ye blessed of my Father, __inherit the kingdom prepared for you__ from the foundation of the world (Rapture or taking up of the elect):... Then shall he say also unto them on his left hand, Depart from me, ye cursed, into everlasting fire, prepared for the Devil and his angels... __And these shall go away into everlasting punishment: but the righteous into life eternal__ (Last Judgment: II Thess. 1:7-10)." (Matt. 25:31-34, 41, 46)

As Christ just indicated, the wicked shall descend into everlasting punishment when He returns. But the righteous shall immediately *"inherit the kingdom prepared for them"*. Naturally, that Kingdom is in Heaven, not on this earth:

"In my Father's house are many mansions: if it were not so, I would have told you. __I go to prepare a place for you__. And if I go to prepare a place for you, I will come again (Second Coming), and

*receive you unto myself; **that where I am (in Heaven), there ye may be also**." (John 14:2-3)*

At Christ's Second Advent judgment is set instantaneously. The Bible states that fact unmistakably. Jesus said:

*"**For the Son of man shall come in the glory of his Father with his angels** (Second Coming; Matt. 24:30-31; Mark 8:38; 13:26-27); **and then he shall reward every man according to his works** (Last Judgment: Rom. 2:6; 14:9-12; I Cor. 3:8; II Cor. 5:10; 11:15; II Tim. 4:14; I Pet. 1:17)." (Matt. 16:27)*

Again it is written:

*"And to you who are troubled rest with us, **when the Lord Jesus shall be revealed** (Gr. apokalupsis; Second Coming: Rom. 8:19; I Cor. 1:7; I Pet. 1:7, 13; 4:13) **from heaven with his mighty angels** (Second Coming: Matt. 24:30-31; Mark 13:26-27), in flaming fire taking vengeance on them that know not God, and obey not the gospel of our Lord Jesus Christ: **Who shall be punished with everlasting destruction** (Last Judgment/ end of time: Matt. 13:40-43, 49-50) from the presence of the Lord, and from the glory of his power; **When he shall come** to be glorified in his saints, and to be admired in all them that believe **in that day**." (II Thess. 1:7-10)*

There's been a "day" appointed by God in which Jesus will judge the world. Paul often spoke of that day. See my notes concerning the day of Christ on page 111. The last judgment, the resurrection, and our Lord's Second Coming all take place on that day:

*"I charge thee therefore before God, and the Lord Jesus Christ, **who shall judge** (Last Judgment: John 12:48) **the quick (living) and the dead** (Resurrection: John 6:39-54) **at his appearing** (Gr. epiphaneia: Second Advent: I Tim. 6:14; II Tim. 1:10) and his kingdom... Henceforth there is laid up for me a crown of righteousness, which the Lord, the righteous judge, shall give me **at that day**: and not to me only, but unto all them also that love his appearing." (II Tim. 4:1, 8)*

That day is also "the last day". The last judgment and resurrection occur at the end of time, not a thousand years before it at the beginning of the millennium. Jesus said:

"He that rejecteth me, and receiveth not my words, hath one that

*judgeth him: the word that I have spoken, **the same shall judge him in the last day**." (John 12:48)*

Christ again:

*"And this is the Father's will which hath sent me, that of all which he hath given me I should lose nothing, **but should raise it up again at the last day** (Resurrection). And this is the will of him that sent me, that every one which seeth the Son, and believeth on him, may have everlasting life: **And I will raise him up at the last day**... No man can come to me, except the Father which hath sent me draw him: **And I will raise him up at the last day** (end of time)... Whoso eateth my flesh, and drinketh my blood, hath eternal life; **And I will raise him up at the last day**." (John 6:39-40, 44, 54)*

Again it is written:

*"Jesus saith unto her, Thy brother shall rise again. Martha saith unto him, I know that **he shall rise again in the resurrection at the last day**." (John 11:23-24)*

Jesus' Second Advent, the final judgment, and the rapture all occur at the very end of time. All of these events are inextricably interwoven. Jesus said:

*"Immediately after the tribulation of those days shall the sun be darkened, and the moon shall not give her light, **and the stars shall fall from heaven** (end of time: II Pet. 3:10-13; Rev. 20:11; 21:1), and the powers of the heavens shall be shaken: And then shall appear the sign of the Son of man in heaven: and then shall all the tribes of the earth mourn, **and they shall see the Son of man coming** (Gr. parousia: Second Coming: I Cor. 15:23; I Thess. 2:19; 3:13; 4:15; 5:23; II Thess. 2:1, 8, 9; James 5:7-8; II Pet. 1:16; 3:4, 12; I John 2:28) in the clouds of heaven (Second Coming: Matt. 26:64; Mark 13:26; 14:62; I Thess. 4:17) with power and great glory. **And he shall send his angels with a great sound of a trumpet**,(Second Coming: I Cor. 15:52; I Thess. 4:16) **and they shall gather together his elect from the four winds** (Rapture: I Thess. 4:17), from one end of heaven to the other." (Matt. 24:29-31) See also Mark 13:24-27.*

The latter takes place at the end of time, not at the beginning of the millennium. Christ sends His angels to gather together His chosen ones at the very end of time, no sooner and no later. Christ Himself said:

*"As therefore the tares are gathered and burned in the fire; **so shall it be in the end of this world. The Son of man shall send forth his angels** (Second Coming: Matt. 24: 31; Mark 13:27), and they shall gather out of his kingdom all things that offend, and them which do iniquity. And shall cast them into a furnace of fire (Last Judgment: II Thess. 1:7-10); there shall be wailing and gnashing of teeth. Then shall the righteous shine forth in the kingdom of their Father." (Matt. 13:40-43)*

Here it is again:

*"**So shall it be at the end of this world: The angels shall come forth** (Second Coming: Matt. 24:30-31; Mark 13:26-27), **and sever the wicked from the just** (Last Judgment: Matt. 25:31-34, 41, 46), and shall cast them into the furnace of fire." (Matt. 13:49-50)*

When Jesus returns, all of His elect are immediately transported to Heaven. This includes those who are dead and those believers who are still alive upon the earth. Once they are in the Kingdom of Heaven they will remain there **forever.** They will not return to this planet to inaugurate the millennium nor for any other reason:

*"For the Lord himself shall descend from heaven with a shout, with the voice of the archangel (Michael; Jude 9), and with the trump(et) of God (Second Advent: Matt. 24:31; I Cor. 15:52): and the dead in Christ shall rise first (Resurrection: John 6:39-40, 44, 54; John 11:23-24; I Cor. 15:52-56): Then we which are alive and remain shall be caught up together with them (Rapture/Assumption) in the clouds (Second Coming: Matt. 24:30; 26:64; Mark 13:26-27; 14:62), to meet the Lord in the air: **And so shall we ever be with the Lord**." (I Thess. 4:16-17)*

All of these things transpire at the end of time. As it is written:

"And at that time shall Michael (the archangel: Jude 9) stand up, the great prince which standeth for the children of thy people: and there shall be a time of trouble, such as never was since there was a nation even to that same time (Tribulation period: Matt. 24:21; Mark 13:19): And at that time thy people shall be delivered, every

*one that shall be found written in the book (Last Judgment: Rev. 20:12). And many of them that sleep in the dust of the earth shall awake (Resurrection: John 6:39-40, 44, 54; 11:23-24; I Cor. 15:52; I Thess. 4:16). Some to everlasting life, and some to shame and everlasting contempt (Last Judgment: Matt. 13:40-42; 25:31-46; Rev. 20:12). And they that be wise shall shine as the brightness of the firmament (end of time: Matt. 13:43); and they that turn many to righteousness as the stars for ever and ever. But thou, O Daniel, shut up the words, and seal the book, **even to the time of the end**: many shall run to and fro, and knowledge shall be increased." (Dan. 12:1-4)*

Anyway, how could Christ reign for a millennium upon this earth if it is utterly vaporized at His Second Coming? St. Peter writes:

*"**But the day of the Lord will come as a thief in the night** (Second Coming: I Thess. 5:2-4); in the which the heavens shall pass away with a great noise, and the elements shall melt with fervent heat, **the earth also and the works that are therein shall be burned up**. Seeing then that all these things shall be dissolved** (end of time: Rev. 20:11; 21:1), what manner of persons ought ye to be in all holy conversation and godliness, Looking for and hasting unto **the coming of the day of God**, wherein the heavens being on fire shall be dissolved, and the elements shall melt with fervent heat? Nevertheless we, according to his promise look for **new heavens and a new earth**, wherein dwelleth righteousness." (II Pet. 3:10-13)* See Amos 9:5 and Micah 1:4.

The end of the world, the last judgment, and the resurrection all take place at the exact same time these *"new heavens and new earth"* are formed. John writes:

*"And I saw a great white throne, and him that sat on it, from whose face the earth and the heaven fled away; and there was found no place for them (end of time: II Pet. 3:10-13). And I saw the dead, small and great, stand before God (Last Judgment: Rom. 14:9-12; II Cor. 5:10); and the books were opened: and another book was opened, which is the book of life (with names of the faithful; Phil. 4:3): **and the dead were judged out of those things which were***

written in the books (end of time/Last Judgment: Dan. 12:1-4; John 12:48), according to their works (Last Judgment: Matt. 3:11-12; 25:31-34; Luke 3:17; John 5:25-29; Rom. 2:4-9; 14:10). And the sea gave up the dead which were in it (Resurrection: John 6:39-40, 44, 54; I Cor. 15:52-56; I Thess. 4:16-17); and death and hell delivered up the dead which were in them: and they were judged every man according to their works (Last Judgment: Matt. 16:27; I Cor. 3:8; II Cor. 11:15; II Tim. 4:14; I Pet. 1:17; Rev 22:12). And death and hell were cast into the lake of fire. This is the second death. And whoever was not found written in the book of life was cast into the lake of fire. And I saw a new heaven and a new earth (end of the world: Isa. 65:17; II Pet. 3:10-13): for the first heaven and the first earth were passed away; and there was no more sea." (Rev. 20:11-14; 21:1)

It is unequivocal; Jesus' Second Coming, the resurrection, the gathering of the elect, the last judgment, and the end of the world all take place at the same time. These Scripture passages are all intertwined and have numerous links connecting them together from all directions. There's not enough room between any two of these events to insert a thousand-year millennium. At our Lord's return, the following events will come to pass simultaneously:

CHRIST'S SECOND COMING SUMMARIZED IN 13 EVENTS

• Jesus returns after the tribulation period: (Matt. 24:29; Mark 13:24; Luke 21:27-28).
• Christ appears with His angels at the sounding of the trumpet: (Matt. 24:31; I Cor. 15:52; I Thess. 4:16).
• Michael the archangel appears: (Dan. 12:1; I Thess. 4:16).
• The resurrection occurs: (Dan. 12:2; John 6:39-40, 44, 54; John 11:23-24; I Cor. 15:52; I Thess. 4:16).
• Christ gathers all nations before Him: (Matt. 25:32).
• Our Lord sends His angels to separate the righteous from the wicked: (Matt. 13:40-43, 49-50; Matt. 25:32-33).

- At that time, the righteous believers will shine as the sun: (Dan. 12:3; Matt. 13:43).
- The mortal bodies of the righteous will be changed to immortal: (I Cor. 15:52-54).
- Christ sends the angels to gather together the elect unto Him: (Matt. 13:41-43, 49; Matt. 24:31; Mark 13:27).
- The believers who will still be alive at our Lord's return shall be caught up into Heaven: (I Thess. 4:17).
- The final judgment: Everyone will be judged according to his own deeds. The elect shall ascend into Heaven; the evil shall descend into hell: (Dan. 12:1-3; Matt. 16:27; Matt. 25:31-46; John 5:27-30; 12:48; Rom. 2:6; 14:9-12; I Cor. 3:8; II Cor. 5:10; 11:15; II Thess. 1:7-10; II Tim. 4:1, 14; I Pet. 1:17; Jude 14-16; Rev. 20:12-13; 22:12).
- All these events come to pass at the very end of time: (Dan. 12:4; Matt. 13:39-43, 49; John 6:39-40, 44, 54; 11:24; 12:48; II Pet. 3:10-13; Rev. 20:11; Rev. 21:1).
- "New Heavens and a New Earth" are formed: (Isa. 65:17; Isa. 66:22; II Pet. 3:13; Rev. 21:1).

This concludes Chapter Nine of my inquiry. Remember, Jesus Christ Himself said: *"My kingdom is not of this world." (John 18:36).*

CHAPTER TEN

THE MILLENNIUM & FALSE CHRISTS

Some time ago I read a book entitled, *Antichrist and the Millennium*, by E. R. Chamberlin. At the time I didn't think much about it. But now as I look back on it, it may have been a little more important than I thought. During the course of the book Mr. Chamberlin cites a few episodes in history when an impostor attempted to impersonate Christ by saying that he had come to introduce the millennium. These impostors had varying degrees of success. It mostly depended upon their capacity to look and act like Jesus. Some were very adroit while others were not so skillful. The point is that some of them were successful at all. But the time is approaching when false christs will come which will have the competence to perform all sorts of flabbergasting miracles.

Some people have been, and still are, teaching that Jesus Christ Himself will descend from Heaven, appear upon earth, and usher in the millennial reign. Any combination of words would surely understate the severity of such an idea. That theory will be, and already is, setting up the supreme stage for the emergence of false christs. If someone could give me an ironclad guarantee that this would not happen I wouldn't have a big problem with it. But nobody has yet done this.

In a book written by the late Herbert Armstrong entitled, *Tomorrow...What it will be Like*, I discovered a very disturbing and frightening proclamation. In the book he claims that when Christ comes to initiate the millennium many people will not believe in Him. He goes on to say that this will occur because Satan's ministers will delude these people into thinking Jesus is the antichrist when He comes. This really alarmed me so I looked into this matter a little further. I found that many rapture and millennium advocates were saying the same kinds of things. I felt that I had to do something about this so I traveled to the Worldwide Church of God in Pasadena, CA. to voice my concerns to him. I didn't get the opportunity to speak with him personally though. Instead, one of his staff members came down to meet with me. He seemed to be knowledgeable about the Bible and the discussion went very well at first. But things quickly began to heat up when I mentioned the dangers of false christs with the millennial concept. When I asked him how he would know the difference between false christs and the real Jesus Christ he floundered and couldn't produce a satisfactory answer. He explained his position by saying that he "would just know". I asked him to be more specific on how he would know and he became very upset and had me escorted off the premises.

Just how are Christians supposed to know whether this person is an impostor or not? Are we to believe he is Jesus simply because a certain well-known individual says he is? When people locate this so-called christ, will they rush to the mountain tops and exclaim: "We have found Christ; We have found Christ! Come and see! He is right over here!"? But Jesus emphatically told us not to believe that any man is Christ no matter what he might say or do.

Yes, our Lord did say He would return after the tribulation period. He further declared that at that precise moment He would send forth His angels to gather together His elect unto Him. But He did not say He was going to descend from Heaven and walk upon the earth in the form of a human being again. Why did He forewarn us of these things? Listen closely to the commonitions of our Lord:

*"Take heed that no man deceive you. For many shall come in my name, saying, I am Christ; and shall deceive many... **Then if any man shall say unto you, Here is Christ, or there: Believe it not**. For there shall arise false Christs, and false prophets, and shall show great signs and wonders; insomuch that, if it were possible, they shall deceive the very elect... Wherefore if they shall say unto you, Behold, he is in the desert; **go not forth**: behold, he is in the secret chambers; **believe it not**." (Matt. 24:4-5, 23-24, 26)*

*"Take heed lest any man deceive you: For many shall come in my name, saying, I am Christ; and shall deceive many... **And then if***

any man shall say unto you, lo, here is Christ; or, lo, he is there; Believe him not: For false Christs and false prophets shall rise, and shall show signs and wonders, to seduce, if it were possible, even the elect. But take ye heed: Behold, I have foretold you all things." (Mark 13:5-6, 21-23)

"Take heed that ye be not deceived: For many shall come in my name, saying, I am Christ; and the time draweth near: go ye not therefore after them." (Luke 21:8)

Why would our Lord command us not to believe that any man is Christ if He knew beforehand that He would be mistaken for a false christ Himself? Jesus certainly wouldn't have told us to consider Him to be a false christ when He returns. And yet, if He was actually going to reappear upon this earth in the form of a man again, that's exactly what He'd be telling us to do. He would be telling us to beware of His own self. What kind of doctrine is this?

When Christ really comes, nobody on this entire planet is going to stand up and call Him a false christ. That already happened to Him once! That's why they crucified Him! **He's not going to take any abuse whatsoever when He Comes!** When Christ really comes **every single living person upon the face of this entire planet will fall down flat!** When our Lord returns in all the might, power, and glory of Almighty God, and the stars are falling from Heaven, and the sun and moon are darkened, and people are rising from the dead and ascending into Heaven, and mighty angels are blasting the trumpet, who do you think is going to stand up, step forward, and blatantly call Him a false christ? This idea is utterly preposterous.

These false christs will probably have a great multitude of diverse followers. Many Jews who believe that the Messiah has not yet come might cleave to them. Many atheists who never before believed on Christ might convert to them also. Many Christians who are unballasted or vacillating in their faith might find them appealing. And if that wasn't enough, many rapture and millennium adherents who profess that Christ will reappear upon the earth again, might embrace them as well: *"Nevertheless when the Son of man cometh, shall he find faith on the earth?"* (Luke 18:8). This is the quintessential element of my argument against the millennium. A false christ is like the epicenter of a proverbial earthquake, violently rocking the very foundations of Christianity and sending out shock waves of false hope in all directions. My friends, hearken to me: No matter how desperately people may try to confute the message of this book, don't allow them to delude you into thinking that Jesus Christ is coming back down upon the earth as a man again.

Just because these false christs will appear altruistic and beneficent doesn't mean they are genuine. Listen once again to the admonition of St. Paul:

*"For such are false apostles, deceitful workers, transforming themselves into the apostles of Christ. And no marvel: For **Satan himself is transformed into an angel of light**. Therefore it is no great thing if his ministers aslo be transformed as ministers of righteousness; whose end shall be according to their works." (II Cor. 11:13-15)*

Some people might think that since God cannot serve Satan and Satan cannot serve God, (Luke 11:17-18), then it would be impossible for a false christ to perform the things I've mentioned. But who's saying God would be serving Satan or the converse? How do you think the followers of this false christ would react if they heard someone irreverently call their Lord an impostor in the presence of everyone? Obviously, Christians who refuse to worship this alleged christ would have to be imprisoned, tortured, or killed. Jesus said it would be our own relatives and best friends that would be doing these things:

*"But before all these, they shall lay their hands on you, and persecute you, delivering you up to the synagogues, and into prisons, being brought before kings and rulers for my name's sake. And it shall turn to you for a testimony. Settle it therefore in your hearts, not to meditate before what ye shall answer: For I will give you a mouth and wisdom, which all your adversaries shall not be able to gainsay nor resist. **And ye shall be betrayed both by parents, and brethren, and kinsfolk, and friends; and some of you shall they cause to be put to death.** And ye shall be hated of all men for my*

*name's sake. " (Luke 21:12-17). See also Matt. 24:9-10; Mark 13:9-
13.*

Remember, this is **during** the great tribulation period. This man
may have already cured many people of terrible plagues or diseases.
He has provided food for starving families by converting rocks into
bread. He has already healed war-torn, burned, or mutilated bodies
with a simple wave of his hand. He appears to be very righteous and
theomorphic. And finally, he claims to be Jesus Christ and has come
to bring in the millennium. Many proponents of the rapture and the
millennium might be standing right next to him proclaiming, "See!
This is the event we spoke of!" The followers of these false christs
would probably think a person to be insane or possessed by a demon
if he disbelieved.

Some people might be wondering: How could these impostors
gain access to such power? When Satan was tempting Jesus in the
wilderness he made the following claim:

*"And the devil, taking him (Jesus) up into a high mountain, showed
unto him all the kingdoms of the world in a moment of time. And the
devil said unto him, **All this power will I give thee, and the glory of
them: For that is delivered unto me; and to whomsoever I will I
give it**. If thou therefore wilt worship me, all shall be thine." (Luke
4:5-7)*

Jesus, of course, did not fall down and worship Satan. But He
also did not dispute Satan's proclamation. The reason is because it
was the truth. Satan is *"the god of this world"*. (See John 12:31;
14:30; II Cor. 4:4; Eph. 6:12). Therefore, it is no great surprise, at
least to me, that these impersonators will be able to perform miracles.
Now these are genuine miracles we're talking about, not cheap tricks
or magical stunts. See my observations about this on pages 81-84.

It is important to remember that when Christ first came, His
miracles were proof of His authenticity. We are reminded of this
many times throughout Scripture: (John 3:2; 7:31; 9:16, 31-33; 10:21,
25, 37-38; 14:11; 15:24; Acts 2:22; 10:38). Here's one example:

*"But I have greater witness than that of John: for the works which
the Father hath given me to finish, **the same works that I do, bear***

witness of me, that the Father hath sent me." (John 5:36)

But Jesus is now telling us that the next time someone "appears" and claims to be Christ his miracles will be concrete evidence against him. This is because our Lord's next appearance will be nothing like His first coming. He is not to return as a lowly human being again, but will return in the might and power of His Father. Both God and Christ are spirits (II Cor. 3:17-18) and we need to worship them in spirit: (John 4:24; I Cor. 15:35-48; Phil. 3:3). Now I'm not saying that anyone who performs miracles is a false christ. Jesus said that as long as we have faith and don't doubt miracles could be performed through the power of God by average Christians, (Mark 11:23-24). I would keep a close eye on anyone who did perform miracles. But as long as he attributes them to the power of God and doesn't claim to be Christ, he is a true Apostle, (II Cor. 12:12).

As far as discerning false christs are concerned, the Apostle John says we should *"try the spirits"* to find out whether or not they are of God:

"Beloved, believe not every spirit, but try the spirits whether they are of God: because many false prophets are gone out into the world." (I John 4:1)

Within the Holy Scriptures we are provided with three fundamental methods for "testing" a prophet. Unfortunately those methods would be insufficient for distinguishing a false christ. Here are those techniques and why they would be useless:

(1). *"When a prophet speaketh in the name of the Lord, if the thing follow not, nor come to pass, that is the thing that the Lord hath not spoken, but the prophet hath spoken it presumptuously: thou shalt not be afraid of him." (Deut. 18:22)*

If a man claims to be a prophet, then every single thing he says must come to pass. There is no room for error. If his predictions come to pass, he is a righteous prophet sent by God. If on the other hand, his predictions fail to transpire, he is specious and is a false minister of Satan.

This method would prove inutile for determining a false christ. Jesus said that these impostors would possess the capability to perform sensational miracles in the sight of men. If this intruder is able to convert rocks into bread I'm sure he will also be able to predict future events. Just because these false christs can predict the future doesn't mean they are sent by God. These could just be enticements used by Satan to convince us that these false christs are authentic. Heed the words of Moses:

*"If there arise among you a prophet, or a dreamer of dreams, and giveth thee a sign or a wonder, **and the sign or the wonder come to pass**, whereof he spake unto thee, saying, **Let us go after other gods** (or false christs), which thou hast not known, and let us serve them; Thou shalt not hearken unto the words of that prophet, or that dreamer of dreams: **For the Lord your God proveth you**, to know whether ye love the Lord your God with all your heart and with all your soul." (Deut. 13:1-3)*

(2). *"And he that keepeth his commandments dwelleth in him, and he in them. And hereby we know that he abideth in us, by the Spirit which he hath given us." (I John 3:23)*

This system also would be inadequate. This is because these impersonators will enjoy the unusual ability to appear supernal in the eyes of others. They might seem to be obedient to God's Holy Commandments, but their thoughts and inner motivations could betray that appearance. Even Lucifer, a name attributed to Satan, means "light". It is apparent, therefore, that it would be quite impossible to characterize this individual as a false christ simply by physiognomy or by examining his actions. Remember, this entity's goal is to inveigle. So he will be very meticulous about what he says or does.

(3). *"Hereby know ye the Spirit of God: Every spirit that confesseth that Jesus Christ is come in the flesh is of God: And every spirit that confesseth not that Jesus Christ is come in the flesh is not of God: and this is that spirit of antichrist, whereof ye have heard that it should come; and even now already is it in the world." (I John 4:2-3)*

This technique would be deficient as well. This is because these imitators could freely admit that Jesus Christ has come in the flesh, but turn right around and claim to be that very same Christ. When our Lord spoke of these false christs, whose name did He say they would come in? He said they *"shall come in my name, saying, I am Christ"*. Not only will these impostors claim to be Christ; but **they will claim to be Jesus Christ**. Otherwise, how could they possibly seduce anyone? If they were to claim to be any other christ than Jesus Christ they would defeat their purpose from the onset; all Christians would automatically know he was a charlatan.

If a person confesses that Jesus has come in the flesh then he is of God. But if the person refuses to acknowledge that Christ has come in the flesh then he is an antichrist. The obvious question then is: "Has Jesus come in the flesh or not?" Of course He did. Jesus already came in the flesh once; He's not coming in the flesh again.

It is paramount to understand that the three latter methods are for distinguishing false prophets, not false christs. Not one of these techniques would suffice for discerning false christs. These intruders will be verisimilitudinous. In other words, they will appear as genuine as the real thing without actually being so. These impersonators could have each and every characteristic of being Christ while He lived on earth but still be a false christ. That's why our Lord warned us about these things.

Well then, just how are we supposed to recognize these false christs? If you see a man and begin to wonder whether he is a false christ or not, simply ask: "Are you Christ?" If he answers affirmatively, he is mendacious; he is both a liar and a false christ. If he declines to answer your question, prevaricates in any way, or allows another to answer for him, he is still a liar and a false christ. Whenever a man is asked if he is the Lord Jesus Christ he must instantly reply: "No! I'm not Christ!" He should not walk away from the scene until he's certain there's not a trace of doubt remaining in the person's mind that asked him the question.

Some people teach that Jesus will return to earth and establish the millennium just when the tribulation period reaches its most critical point. They declare that Jesus will come down upon earth when mankind is on the very brink of annihilating himself. According to them this will be God's way of *"shortening"* this period of suffering, (Matt. 24:22). I think it is far more than a mere ironic coincidence that the very next verse says: *"Then if any man shall say unto you, Lo, here is Christ, or there, believe it not."* (Matt. 24:23). It seems like Jesus knew in advance that people would be using His own words to introduce these impostors.

Some chiliasts (millennium teachers) might protest: "But when Christ comes He will be seen by everyone." If so they are contradicting their own doctrine. Why do many of them say people will not believe him? When Jesus really comes we will no longer have the choice to believe or disbelieve anything. Certainly no mortal is going to stand up and call Him a false christ when He comes. If such a thought even entered the mind of anyone (which I find totally incomprehensible), that individual would be **obliterated** before the words even left his mouth!

Just to say that Jesus Christ is coming back down upon the earth is a dangerous concept to preach. After experiencing such hard times how many people would even care how He appears? This would be especially true of rapture and millennium supporters. After going through such terrifying times who couldn't use a miracle or two? Who has seen a miracle performed? Just think how astounding it would be to witness one. Keep in mind these wonders will have a greater impact when there is a **need** for them. If our children are hungry, this invader could provide us with food. If our bodies are disfigured, burned, or fatigued, he could rejuvenate them. Any thing we may need could be provided by this false christ. Even if someone had a doubt about him it would be very easy "to look the other way". Especially if his own face is transmogrified or his own children are starving.

Many Christians are awaiting the arrival of the antichrist of the apocalypse whose number is 666. But will false christs be that perceptible? How could they deceive the very elect if that were possible? Will these false christs walk around with "666" plastered all over them? I can't think of a number which is more widely recognized than that number! Even many unbelievers are aware of what that number represents. These impostors are going to do every thing possible to disassociate themselves with that number. I suggest people be more careful about making hasty suppositions concerning the Revelation. It seems Satan has gotten many scholars on the wrong track. They've got their heads buried so far into the Revelation that they can't extract them long enough to see the truth. My readers will understand my position after reading the next chapter.

Another thing to keep in mind is that our Lord is not talking about antichrists; He is talking about false christs. There's a big difference. Antichrist simply means "against Christ". There are many antichrists in the world today, (I John 2:18, 22). An atheist is an antichrist. But a false christ is a totally different thing. A false christ is claiming to be Jesus Christ Himself. The distinction being thus: An antichrist is not necessarily a false christ and doesn't necessarily have the power to perform miracles. But a false christ is an antichrist and may possess the capability to perform all sorts of signs, wonders, and miracles.

Of course, if anyone attempts to force you into receiving the number 666 or any other mark upon your flesh you should adamantly resist and refuse it no matter what the consequences might be. The Bible forbids this practice:

*"Ye shall not make any cuttings in your flesh for the dead, **nor print any marks upon you**: I am the Lord." (Lev. 19:28)*

I find it extremely unlikely that the practice of marking people with 666 or any other marks will ever be instituted. If there were an attempt to do so there would be a worldwide religious uprising unprecedented in the history of mankind. There are more than a billion Christians upon the face of the earth who would not be very happy about this. The Jews also would refuse to submit to this. The Qur'an does not address this question directly, but I greatly doubt the Muslims would accept it either. The Muslims and Jews are half-brothers (same father/ different mother) and I doubt they would differ on this point. I'm sure there are some that would contend against that statement and say that the Muslims and Jews are actually cousins. But this would be true only if we go back as far as the Children of Israel. The ancestral lineage of the Jews does not stop there. In order to accurately trace the genealogy of the Jews we need to take it one step further. The Jews are actually the descendents of Isaac while the Muslims are the descendents of Ishmael. And they are both the sons of Abraham. At any rate, they both regard the laws set down by Moses as dear and holy unto them.

I suppose there's a very strong possibility that I will be labeled a "false minister of Satan". Mr Armstrong's statement already does. But I am not concerned about what others think of me. I'm supposed to give my testimony, not be a coward. My primary concern is to get this written, circulated, and acknowledged. It would be more likely for the chair I'm sitting in to slide out from under me and walk away than for me to abandon my goal of finishing this project.

This concludes Chapter Ten of my investigation. Remember, we live by faith, not by sight.

CHAPTER ELEVEN

TAMPERING WITH THE REVELATION

Many rapture and millennium advocates construct great portions of their theories from the symbolical prophecies contained within the book of Revelation. This could be a big mistake. The apocalypse is definitely one of the most difficult books of the Bible to understand. This is due to the multiplicity of interrelated elements and the complexity of the symbols contained therein. I'm not saying that just because I personally find it difficult to comprehend. But it is mysterious and inscrutable for every single person who ever sat down and read it. Unless, of course, the reader is genuinely vaticinal. Spiritual symbolism is not something that can be found out by exhaustive research alone. In order to ascertain the meanings of these symbols, we absolutely require divine assistance. Adam Clarke sums up the matter quite well when he writes:

"My readers will naturally expect that I should either give a decided preference to some one of the opinions stated above, or produce one of my own; I can do neither, nor can I pretend to explain the book (of Revelation): I do not understand it; and in the things which concern so sublime and awful a subject, I dare not, as my predecessors, indulge in conjectures. I have read elaborate works on the subject, and each seemed right till another was examined. I am satisfied that no certain mode of interpreting the prophecies of this book has yet been found out, and I will not add another monument to the littleness or folly of the human mind by endeavoring to strike out a new course. I repeat it, I do not understand the book; and I am satisfied that not one who has written on the subject knows any more of it than myself. A conjecture concerning the design of the book may be safely indulged; thus then it has struck me, that the book of the Apocalypse may be considered as a prophet continued in the Church of God, uttering predictions relative to all times, which have their successive fulfillment as ages roll on; and thus it stands in the Christian Church in the place of the succession of prophets in the Jewish Church; and by this especial economy prophecy is still continued, is always speaking; and yet a succession of prophets rendered unnecessary. If this be so, we cannot too much admire the wisdom of the contrivance which still continues the voice and testimony of prophecy, by means of a very short book, without the assistance of any extraordinary messenger, or any succession of such messengers, whose testimony would at all times be liable to suspicion, and be the subject of infidel and malevolent criticism, however unexceptionable to ingenious minds the credentials of such might appear. On this ground it is reasonable to suppose that several prophecies contained in this book have been already fulfilled, and that therefore it is the business of the commentator to point such out. It may be so; but as it is impossible for me to prove that my conjecture is right, I dare not enter into proceedings upon it, and must refer to Bishop Newton, and such writers as have made this their particular study… My readers will therefore excuse me from any exposure of my ignorance or folly by attempting to do what many, with much more wisdom and learning, have attempted, and what every man to the present day has failed in, who has preceded me in expositions of this book. I have no other mountain to heap on those already piled up; and if I had, I have not strength to lift it: those who have courage may again make the trial; already we have had a sufficiency of vain efforts… Shall I have the readers pardon if I say that it is my firm opinion that the expositions of this book have done great disservice to religion: **Almost every commentator has become a prophet; for as soon as he began to explain he began also to prophesy**. And what has been the issue? Disappointment laughed at hope's career, and superficial thinkers have been led to despise and reject prophecy itself." (Clarke's Commentary, Vol. 6; pp 965-967).

Does he say it like it is or what? It's too bad we all didn't approach this topic the way Mr. Clarke did. If we all did we wouldn't be faced with the dumpster full of erroneous arguments we are faced with today. You'd think people would have learned that by now. But sadly that definitely is not the case.

Many people are stating conjecture and speculation as incontrovertible fact. They are attempting to convert their own concepts into the precepts of God. This is a very perilous practice, especially when formulating expositions concerning symbolical prophecy. Many theologians and Bible scholars seem to have the tendency to declare that they **know** the meanings of the symbols in the apocalypse. Also, these self-made conclusions are hammered into the hearts and minds of naïve and vulnerable Christians. This propagates confusion. No man knows the meanings of the symbols in the Book of Revelation. One can only guess as to the matter. Constructing a formidable hypothesis is a lot different than claiming it to be fact. These individuals are not merely claiming perspicacity; but clairvoyance. When a person claims to know the meanings of symbolical prophecy he is implicitly claiming to be a prophet.

The apocalypse is an excellent example of this perplexing paradox. There are approximately 12,000 words of symbolical prophecy contained within the Revelation and many people claim to understand it all. They don't say: "This is what it **could** mean". Or: "This is what it **might** mean". Or: "This is what I **think** it means". Or even: "This is what it **probably** means". They say: "This is **precisely** what it means". This kind of reasoning is pansophistic and insalubrious. We should be a lot more careful about what we say regarding these prophecies.

Who has discovered the infinite? The infinitesimal? Within an infinitesimal piece of matter there is an infinite number of things to know about it. For example: Imagine an atom as a hollow sphere. Roughly a million billion nuclei could be placed within its circumference. (I speak according to the knowledge of man: *The Collapsing Universe*, by Isaac Asimov, pg. 8). If we are unable to fully comprehend corporeal things, how can we fully comprehend symbolical prophecy, a spiritual matter? Is it possible for a mere man to establish and determine, without imperfection, the meanings of symbolical prophecy, the Holy Word of God?

Who knows the difference between the boundary and the

boundless? The shortest and the longest? The tallest and the smallest? These are simply limitations of man's understanding. Nothing is limited. Therefore, everything is limitless. The tallest can always get taller and the smallest can always get smaller. Forget the Schwarzschild radius. This is just another one of man's theories which is impossible for him to comprehend or prove. No matter how small something gets, it can always be cut in half. Only the Lord can know the Schwarzschild radius of a thing. He has created all things, including time. He was before time came into being and will remain when it is over. He can take a thing that exists and make it as though it never did. And take a thing that never existed and make it as though it always has, (cf. I Cor. 1:28). What is one day in the mind of man compared to eternity? No matter how expansive eternity becomes and how infinitesimal the day becomes in comparison, does it not remain existent? The day, fleeting though it may be, will never disappear altogether. In that one day 5,000 people may have been born into the world. That one day is not so inconsequential if one of those people happen to be you. With all our limitations and imperfections innate within us, is it responsible to declare that we know the meanings of the complex symbols of the apocalypse?

Consider the mathematical number line: We have positive and negative numbers traveling infinitely in opposite directions. They will never meet so long as they travel this way. But don't they also travel infinitely toward each other? The negative numbers can travel decimally endlessly toward the positive; while the positive numbers can travel decimally endlessly toward the negative. No matter how close they get they will never actually meet. Because to do so transforms the negative numbers into the positive and the positive numbers into the negative. And no matter how much the value of '0' is crushed between them it will always be there. The value of '0' therefore, becomes an infinity in itself even though it has circumscribed limitations. This is why the value of pi has never been ascertained. There's no beginning or ending to the geometrical figure of a circle. For as soon as we assign a beginning to it and draw a perfect arc back upon itself, it can never meet with the point of origin again. As the value of pi infinitely increases, the gap between these two points infinitely decreases. But they will never actually meet. Because to do so transforms the end of the arc into the beginning and the beginning of the arc into the ending. What we really have then is a ray bent into an arc which has a beginning (only because we've assigned one to it) but no ending because it can never meet with the point of origin again. For the point of origin to meet with the point of destination is to go too far. But for these two points not to meet at all doesn't go far enough and leaves the circle incomplete. This disproves the Schwarzschild radius and solves the mathematical riddle of pi at the same time. Over time man has come to believe that he can ascertain the circumference of any given circle. But in reality this is just an illusion because his logic is based upon an approximation. This is exactly what has happened with symbolical prophecy. Man has come to believe he can decipher the meanings of symbolical prophecy through exhaustive research. But this is just an illusion because all his complex and fascinating theories are founded upon conjecture and speculation. Hence, his idea remains imperfect and incomplete. *"It is the glory of the Lord to conceal a thing"* (Prov. 25:2). And if the Lord has hidden a thing, who can find it out?

Now consider just a few symbols of the apocalypse: the seven golden candlesticks, the twenty-four elders in Heaven, the four beasts in Heaven, the book sealed with seven seals, the lion and the lamb, the four horseman, the 144,000 sealed, the seven angels with the seven trumpets, the angel and the little book, the two witnesses of God, the sun-clad woman, the great red dragon, the man child, the war in Heaven with Michael, the first beast with seven heads and ten horns, the ten crowns on the ten horns, the second beast with a mortal wound, the harvest of the Earth, the seven vials of wrath, the fall of Babylon, the marriage supper of the lamb, the rider on the white horse, the beast and the false prophet cast into the lake of fire, Satan bound a thousand years with a chain, Satan released from his prison after the thousand-year confinement, the first resurrection and the second death, Gog and Magog, the judgment at the great white throne, and the creation of a new Heaven, new Earth, and a new Jerusalem, etc. Another thing to bear in mind is that this is all a vision, John seeing all these things in the Spiritual world! Now let's be reasonable: Is it responsible to say we **know** the meanings of all these things? Or is it more responsible to admit we are guessing?

Now I'm not saying we should refrain from guessing as to the meanings of symbolical prophecy. I am saying, however, that we had better be careful about what we say concerning them. If we state our guesses as guesses, we will be safe. If, on the other hand, we state our guesses as irrefutable truth, we are in grave danger of being condemned. To those who wish to indulge in such practices the Bible warns that they had better be absolutely correct about every single thing they say, (Deut. 4:2; Prov. 30:5-6; Rom.1:22). Isaiah reminds us:

"Woe unto them that call evil good, and good evil: that put darkness for light, and light for darkness; that put bitter for sweet, and sweet for bitter! Woe unto them that are wise in their own eyes, and prudent in their own sight." (Isa. 5:20-21)

The apocalypse is the **only book of the Bible** that explicitly warns its readers not to meddle with its message or meaning;

"For I testify unto every man that heareth the words of the prophecy of this book, If any man shall add unto these things, God shall add unto him the plagues that are written in this book: And if any man shall take away from the words of the book of this prophecy, God shall take away his part out of the book of life, and out of the holy city, and from the things which are written in this book." (Rev. 22:18-19)

Is it worth the risk? 99.9 % correct is not correct enough. For what part does imperfection have with perfection? For what part does darkness have with light? If you sprinkle a little salt into a pot of soup as large as the Atlantic Ocean, does the soup have salt in it? *"A little leaven leaveneth the whole lump"*, (I Cor. 5:6; Gal. 5:9).

A long time ago I, too, had fallen into this trap. It's not that hard to do. I began to consider myself an "authority" on symbolical prophecy. I thought that I had finally figured out the meanings of the apocalypse. After all, I had studied it so intensely and had read every book about it I could get my hands on. Shortly thereafter, I found that my interpretations seemed more important to me than the truth. All I looked for was Scriptural passages that supported my theory. Occasionally, I discovered a few "very small phrases" that presented obstacles for my theory. In time I found myself simply overlooking those passages. The proof for my theory was so overwhelming that I thought it would be "acceptable" to disregard some little aspect here or there. Then, and I thank the Lord God, I considered these things introspectively. I began to see these things in their proper perspectives. I realized there was no such thing as a "trivial technicality" when considering symbolical prophecy. I realized I was wrong for doing that which I had been doing. After all, close was not nearly close enough.

I began to understand and appreciate the meanings of such words as "theory", "hypothesis", "opinion", "view", etc. I realized these terms were created for a definitive purpose. They are reserved for the time when one is not absolutely certain of his proposition. Therefore he applies one of the latter terms to it to circumvent improvidence. He labels his thought a theory rather than fact to remain safe. For he never knows when someone might stand up, confute his self-made "fact", and publicly rebuke and humiliate him. If someone steps forward and disproves a person's theory, what then, has he lost? He has lost nothing. Instead, he gains wisdom and knowledge and is not rebuked. This individual was not found to be unwise because he never declared that he knew in the beginning.

What does all this have to do with the millennium? It is from the Revelation that this idea was originally conceived. There is no strong evidence for it anywhere else in the Bible. It is not mentioned in the Gospels, nor the Epistles, which are far less ambiguous. I want my readers to realize that nobody completely understands this complicated book. Hence, any theory fabricated from it is quite worthy of skepticism and quite unworthy of unfaltering belief. I want my readers to understand that there are many more ways than one to look at, interpret, and consider the apocalypse. For this reason I am compelled to venture into something that I did not initially intend to do. I will provide here, with reluctance, a very brief summary of my thoughts on the millennium. I can't help but feel like I'm going to regret this risky undertaking. I already do and I haven't even started yet. I will make this as brief as possible. When I first began writing this book, one of my main goals was to keep it Scripturally sound, preferring to keep my opinions out of it. In doing what I'm about to do, I feel like I'm "cutting against the grain". This makes me a little uncomfortable. But it doesn't diminish my argument. If I can show that there are other plausible explanations for the millennium, then this will supplement rather than subtract from my argument.

I suppose it goes without saying that I cannot prove my theory and I'm certainly not attempting to. I've accumulated a pile of handwritten notes three feet thick and a ton of books about this subject. But I still don't know any more about the apocalypse than the next guy. I can't remember the exact moment I came to this realization. But I do remember that I was extremely disheartened when I did. It took nearly twenty years of hard work and research to find out this one thing: I don't **know** what I'm talking about. Like Mr. Clarke's observations I nearly began to despise symbolic prophecy altogether. Finally and fortunately I understood what the whole mess was about. I realized I didn't have to **prove** anything. This was one tremendous weight off my shoulders. Hopefully my readers will give it a try and see what I mean. I will not attempt to prove that my theory is right. Instead, I will prove that it could be. In so doing I will make my point: That the Revelation means many different things to many different people. There are good Christians on all sides of this issue and there's nothing wrong with that as long as they promote edification of the Church, (I Cor. 14:26-33; II Pet. 1:20). But if any of these opinions divide the Church, or possesses an element of danger, especially one as serious as false christs, then they are worthy only of the trash bin.

First of all, I feel the millennium is a spiritual kingdom, not a literal physical kingdom upon this Earth. I have two fundamental reasons for this. We've discussed the first one already: The fact that if this is interpreted literally, we are faced with the prospect of false christs. Secondly, a literal millennial kingdom upon this earth contradicts Christ's own words: *"My kingdom is not of this world"*, (John 18:36). After all, an angel descends from Heaven to bind Satan, not Christ, (Rev. 20:1). These passages say nothing about our Lord reigning upon this earth. Those who reign for this thousand years do so with Christ, not He with them. And where is Christ? Jesus said:

*"And I say unto you, That many shall come from the east and the west, and shall sit down with Abraham, and Isaac, and Jacob, **in the kingdom of heaven**." (Matt. 8:11)*

Every time Jesus spoke of His Kingdom, He always said it was a Heavenly Kingdom. See: (Matt. 3:2; 4:17; 5:10, 12, 19, 20; 7:21; 10:7; 11:11, 12; 13:11, 24, 31, 33, 44, 45, 47, 52; 18:1, 3, 4, 23; 19:12, 14, 23, 24; 20:1; 22:2; 23:13; 25:1, 34; 26:29; Mark 9:47; Luke 13:28, 29; 14:15; 22:30; 23:42).

It is also important to bear in mind that these prophecies were deliberately left "unsealed". In other words, many of the predictions of the Revelation were to transpire near the time it was composed. Indeed, some of the events within were probably already occurring:

*"The Revelation of Jesus Christ, which God gave unto him, to show unto his servants **things which must shortly come to pass**; and he sent and signified it by his angel unto his servant John... Blessed is he that readeth, and they that hear the words of this prophecy, and keep those things which are written therein: **For the time is at hand**... Write the things which thou hast seen, **and the things which are**, and the things which shall be hereafter;" (Rev. 1:1, 3, 19)*

The Revelation again:

*"And he said unto me, These sayings are faithful and true: and the Lord God of the holy prophets sent his angel to show unto his servants **the things which must shortly be done**... And he saith unto me, **seal not the sayings of the prophecy of this book: For the time is at hand**." (Rev. 22:6, 10)*

With these statements glaring back at me from the apocalypse it's very difficult for me to believe that none of the predictions therein have taken place within the last twenty centuries.

I think those who reign with Christ during the millennium are those who were martyred for His name by the heathen Roman Empire. These persecutions firmly established and built the Church upon a sure foundation, the cornerstone of which is our Lord Jesus Christ: John writes:

"And I saw thrones, and they sat upon them, and judgment was given unto them: <u>And I saw the souls of them that were beheaded for the witness of Jesus</u>, and for the word of God, <u>and which had not worshiped the beast</u>, neither his image, neither had received his mark upon their foreheads, or in their hands; and they lived and reigned with Christ a thousand years." (Rev. 20:4)

This is very interesting. Those who reign during the millennium are an elite little group of martyrs. So unless a person is executed for his testimony of Christ Jesus he should not expect nor hope to rule during this period of time. This immediately excludes a great deal of Christians, both past and present. We must keep this in mind when we think about the millennium and those accounted worthy to reign during it.

Additionally, those who reign for the millennium are those who refused to worship the beast, or receive his mark, and have been executed for that reason. This gives us another clue as to whom John is referring. I think it is awfully coincidental that the Roman Empire and two of its most notorious rulers (Nero and Teitan) can be linked directly to the number of the beast (666). This would explain why John might have felt it necessary to use numerical figures to depict the people he was writing about. St. John was probably taking advantage of the fact that the letters of both the Hebrew and Greek alphabets were assigned numerical values. By using this method of naming people with numbers (called gematria), St. John could divulge the identities of these individuals without risking further persecution.

The values of Nero's name are: 50+200+6+50+100+60+200=666. The values of Teitan's name are: 300+5+10+300+1+50=666. The values for the Roman Empire are: 30+1+300+5+10+50+70+200=666. To examine this further refer to *Clarke's Commentary*, Vol. 6; pages 964, 1,026 and *Antichrist and the Millennium*, by E.R. Chamberlin,

155

pg. 17. There are many books in your local library that address this topic and draw the same conclusion. And almost every commentator who has studied the apocalypse will agree that the mystic Babylon of Revelation 14:8; 16:19; Chs. 17 & 18 is probably the city of Rome which *"stood on seven mountains"*, (Rev. 17:9). There are a few other clues in the Revelation that point in this direction. But I won't list them now. I want this to be brief.

The idea that the beast represents the Roman Empire and its tyrannical rulers was widely accepted by the Christians of the time. We also know that many of the Caesars required obeisance from those they ruled over. Some of them even required their subjects to actually fall down and worship them as gods. Those who refused were often executed. We know from history and Scripture that thousands upon thousands of Christians were slaughtered by the Roman Empire. It wasn't until Constantine overthrew the Roman Empire in the fourth century that these practices were finally abolished. I think this is when the millennium began. This idea was generally embraced by Christians of the time as well as Constantine himself. We can imagine how much of a relief it must have been for Christianity as a whole to be able to practice their religious beliefs without risking their lives. Constantine was the first Christian Emperor that not only allowed Christians to worship, but encouraged it. He tore down the temples of the pagan gods of Rome and replaced them with Christian Churches effectively establishing Christianity as the national religion. Adam Clarke comments:

"It is very remarkable, that Constantine himself, and the Christians of his time, describe his conquests **under the image of a dragon**, as if they understood that this prophecy (Rev. 13) had received its accomplishment in him. Constantine himself, in his epistle to Eusebius and other bishops concerning the re-edifying and repairing of the churches, saith that 'liberty being now restored, **and the dragon being removed** from the administration of public affairs, by the providence of the great God to have been made manifest to all'. Moreover, a picture of Constantine was set up over the palace gate, with the cross over his head, and under his feet the great enemy of mankind, who persecuted the Church by means of impious tyrants, **in the form of a dragon**, transfixed with a dart through the midst of his body, and falling headlong into the depth of the sea."

"And it is certain that the Roman Empire under Constantine the Great was the brightest emblem of the latter day glory which has ever yet been exhibited to the world. It is well known that sun, moon, and stars are emblems, in prophetic language, of empires, kingdoms, and states. And as the morning star is that which immediately precedes the rising of the sun, it probably here intends an empire which should usher in the universal sway of the kingdom of Christ. Ever since the time of Constantine the light of true religion has been increasingly diffused, and is shining more and more unto the perfect day." (Clarke's Commentary, Vol. 6; pp. 1,019 & 982)

We see from these excerpts that Constantine as well as the Christians of his time felt that the millennium had been initialized at the beginning of his reign.

What about the binding of Satan? I don't think that just because Satan is restricted from deceiving mankind that sin would be abolished from the face of the earth altogether. Sin is inherent in man. Did Satan force Adam and Eve to consume the forbidden fruit? No, they sinned even before they actually ate the fruit by doubting the Word of the Lord. This was their own doing, not Satan's.

For a millennium after the fall of Rome mankind wandered aimlessly upon the face of the earth. There were very little or no advancements in science, philosophy, or technology. Man basically "sat still in time" upon the earth during this thousand years. This period of time is referred to as the Dark Ages or the Middle Ages. And it is common knowledge that historians have traditionally dated the beginning of the Middle Ages at the fall of the Roman Empire in 325 A.D. and this age of "intellectual darkness" prevailed for approximately 1,000 years.

But isn't the millennium supposed to perdure for one thousand years exactly? Not necessarily. Numbers, especially large ones, were often rounded off in the Bible. For example, God told Abraham that his ancestors would be held in bondage to the Egyptians for 400 years, (Gen. 15:13). But they actually remained there for 430 years, (Gal. 3:17). Of course, there are alternative ways of interpreting this mystical number. If we were to extrapolate the millennium's duration in the prophetic terms of Daniel, a day for a year (Dan. 9:24-27), we end up with a millennial reign of 365,000 years. Or if we interpret this using the simile employed by St. Peter, *"a day is as a thousand years and a thousand years as one day,"* (II Pet. 3:8), we have a millennium enduring anywhere from one day to 365 million years! Of course, these calculations don't fit very well into my theory. But that doesn't make them any less possible.

The point is that the millennium doesn't essentially last for precisely 1,000 years. This might well be an estimation. But what happened to Christianity during this period of time? First of all persecution ceased. The Church grew strong, organized, and unified. The false teachings of antinomianism were suppressed. And as we near the end of the thousand years Christianity was veritably forced upon people by those famous (or infamous if you prefer) conquests commonly referred to as the Crusades. I realize this may seem like a severe tactic for expanding Christianity. But it expanded nonetheless. This is not the first nor only time Christianity was forced upon someone. What about Paul? He persecuted the Church exceedingly before he was blinded by Christ. It wasn't until his conversion to Christianity three days later that his sight was restored to him, (Acts 9:1-18). Paul became an Apostle of our Lord *"by the will of God"*, not by his own, (II Cor. 1:1; Gal. 1:15; Eph. 1:1; Col. 1:1; II Tim. 1:1).

Now I'm not defending the Crusades nor advocating the tactics utilized during them. But I am not condemning them either. How do I know this wasn't God's will? Some people might think these practices were implacable and were too severe under any circumstances, or for achieving any goals, no matter how magnanimous the cause. People should be more careful about what they say when they speak about God and His mysterious ways. Many times He sent the Israelites into battle and told them to kill every single male; this included toddlers and infants. (See Num. 31:17-18;

Judges 21:10-11; I Sam. 15:3). Can you imagine the sight of Israel's mighty men of war riding through town hacking babies to death? I'm always very careful about what I say about these things. Who am I that I should enter into judgment with the Lord God? Remember, I'm not saying the Crusades were the will of God. But since I don't know for sure, I am restrained from denouncing them. I didn't live back then and I have no idea what these people were thinking, so it's not my place to make these determinations.

I also want my readers to know that I am not attempting to defend Catholicism either. If I were, I certainly wouldn't be using these arguments to do so. The abuses of the Church during the Middle Ages are well documented and not even the Catholic Church would deny that, especially near the end of this thousand years with the selling of indulgences. But it is definitely worthy to note that there was only one Church of Christ for nearly 1,500 years. But I don't have the time to tackle this issue now.

Now let's address the question of Satan's release. Almost exactly 1,000 years after the fall of Rome a most dreadful plague struck the inhabitants of the earth, (325 A.D. to 1347 A.D.). This is the Black Plague or Black Death of the fourteenth century. It would only seem logical that something so cataclysmic would take place upon Satan's release. (I realize my logical reasoning is nonsense to God. Remember, this is a theory). Something like one-third of the world's entire population was wiped out by the Plague. The Church lost a lot of its respect and power because the clergy were falling down dead as fast as the common man. Schism fragmented the Church as antinomianism once again reared its ugly head. But mankind bounced back from this catastrophe as though nothing had happened. Art, science, philosophy, and technology began to develop rapidly. Discovery and exploration of the world began almost instantaneously. Man began to branch out in every aspect of life. This period of time is referred to by historians as the Renaissance or Reformation. I think this marks the release of Satan upon the earth. Some people claim this marks the beginning of "modern civilization". Maybe it does. But the same technology that gave us all the conveniences we now enjoy also gave us air pollution, ozone depletion, deforestation, global warming, water pollution, toxic waste, and the hydrogen bomb! Call it "advancement" if you like.

As for the resurrection of the martyrs that is expected, just because these individuals are resurrected from the grave and ascended into Heaven doesn't mean anyone would have had to witness the event. When our Lord was on the cross He turned to the man next to Him and said: *"To day shalt thou be with me in paradise."* (Luke 23:42-43). But it doesn't essentially follow that anyone actually saw him go there. It's also a known fact that shortly after our Lord's crucifixion the graves of the saints were opened and they appeared to many people in Jerusalem, (Matt. 27:52-53). Maybe this was a prelude to the "first resurrection"? (Rev. 20:5)

I have one more reason why I feel the millennium may have occurred already. It concerns the battle with Gog and Magog after the millennium. Anyone who has already read any books about this matter can probably surmise where I'm going with this. But this requires rather lengthy scrutiny. Hence, I have reserved a separate chapter to address that issue.

I have been as compendious as possible. I could dig up tons of material to bolster my hypothesis. I could write a capacious book on this subject alone. In fact, I already have a large box full of research material on this topic. Nowadays it just sits around collecting dust. I can't count how many times I've stubbed my toe on the thing! How ironic, what was once a stumbling block figuratively has now become one literally. I'd throw it in the garbage if it hadn't taken so much time to accumulate. One of these days I might pull it out and assemble a better organized thesis on this matter. But I doubt it. My hands are tied until I can get this project finished. So I'm not going to toy with this subject any further. I'm glad it's over. I've been lying awake all night dreading this adventure. It sure is nice not having to prove my conjecture. I merely wanted to illustrate the fact that there are alternative ways of considering the millennium.

When we don't know or understand a thing why should we be embarrassed to admit it? Confucius once said: "When you do not

know a thing, to acknowledge that you do not know it is knowledge".
The Holy Bible says: *"He that answereth a matter before he hears
(or knows) it, it is folly and shame unto him."* (Prov. 18:13).

It is unwise to claim to know something when, in fact, you don't
know it. If you harbor any doubt you shouldn't claim to know it, (cf.
I Cor. 8:2). If a world history teacher claims to know a thing and is
incorrect, he only stands to lose a little integrity. But if a Bible teacher
claims to know a thing and is incorrect, he stands to lose his own
soul and the souls of all those who believe what he says, (cf. I Tim.
4:16; James 3:1-2).

Many people are declaring that they **know** the millennium will
take place upon earth and in the very near future. They say it is
imminent because the signs of the tribulation period are fast
approaching. And since this millennium purportedly transpires just
after this period of time, then it must be very near, even perhaps,
right around the turn of the century. But the Holy Bible denounces
this kind of reasoning because no man can foretell the future without
direct divine assistance, (Ecc. 3:22)

It is imperative when we make inferences about the meanings of
the apocalypse that we declare **openly** that we are merely speculating
as to the matter. This is especially true with Bible teachers. Otherwise,
their pupils might get the silly idea that the teacher knows what he's
talking about. The only thing known about the Revelation is that
nobody knows exactly what it means. We don't know precisely when
it was written. We don't know who wrote it, John the Evangelist,
John the Apostle, etc. We don't know if it's written in chronological
order. We don't know which portions should be interpreted
tropologically. We don't know which ones should be interpreted
literally. We don't which portions may be ambiguous and possess
more than one meaning. We don't know for certain what the symbols
represent. We don't know which predictions may have been fulfilled
already. We don't know which predictions have yet to be fulfilled.
And finally, we don't know which events are to transpire in the
physical world and which ones are to occur in the Spiritual world.

CHAPTER TWELVE

THE EVERLASTING KINGDOMS

I've noticed that many chiliasts frequently utilize such Old Testament prophecies as Dan. 7:13-14 to corroborate their theories: *"I saw in the night visions, and, behold, one like the Son of man came with the clouds of heaven, and came to the Ancient of days, and they brought him near before him. And there was given him (Christ) dominion, and glory, and a kingdom (supposedly the Millennium), that all people, nations, and languages, should serve him:* **His dominion is an everlasting dominion, which shall not pass away, and his kingdom that which shall not be destroyed.** *"*

We know that this reading deals with the coming of Jesus Christ, (cf. Psa. 2:6-8; Eze. 1:26; Matt. 24:30; 28:18; John 3:35; I Cor. 15:27; Eph. 1:22; Rev. 1:7). But this passage certainly does not concern the millennium. That's simply because the millennium does not prevail indefinitely. Like I said before this might well be an estimation. Although we are not absolutely sure of the millennium's duration we are sure it has circumscribed limitations. It has both a beginning and an ending. It begins with the confinement of Satan and discontinues with his release. However, I have often seen these interminable kingdoms of the Old Testament pointed out as if they pertained to the millennial reign. I refer to these prophecies as "the Everlasting Kingdoms". If a certain state or condition is to persist "for ever", "for evermore", "without end", "everlasting", etc. then that prediction has nothing to do with the millennium because it does not last forever.

The Old Testament is replete with references to these "Everlasting Kingdoms". Consult the following list for just a few more examples: (Gen. 13:15; Ex. 32:13; Josh. 14:9; II Sam. 7:13, 16; I Kings 9:3; I Chr. 17:14; 23:25; 28:7; II Chr. 13:5; 20:6-7; Ezra 9:12; Psa. 18:50; 37:27-28; 89:28; 132:12; 133:3; Prov. 29:14; Isa. 2:4; 9:7; 32:17;

34:17; 55:13; 56:5; 60:20; 61:8; Jer. 7:7; 17:25; 25:5; 31:40; 32:39-40; Eze. 16:60; 37:25; 43:7, 9; Dan. 7:27; 9:24; 12:2; Hos. 2:18-19; Joel 3:20; Micah 4:7).

Another thing to remember is that this Earth is transitory; it doesn't endure forever either. It is utterly destroyed after the conflict with Gog and Magog, (Rev. 20:11 & 21:1). Even our Lord Jesus Christ said: *" Heaven and earth shall pass away, but my words shall not pass away"*, (Matt. 24:35). The Bible says:

"Love not the world, neither the things that are in the world. If any man love the world, the love of the Father is not in him. For all that is in the world, the lust of the flesh, and the lust of the eyes, and the pride of life, is not of the Father, but is of the world. And the world passeth away, and the lust thereof: but he that doeth the will of God abideth for ever." (I John 2:15-17).

The fact that this Earth is to be destroyed is a well-known Biblical theme. For further references of this, see: (Psa. 50:3-6; 102:25-26; Isa. 24:1-23; 34:4; 51:6; 66:15-24; Joel 2:31; I Cor. 7:31; II Thess. 1:6-10; Heb. 1:10-12; I Pet. 1:24; 4:7; II Pet. 3:3-15).

It seems to me that these "Everlasting Kingdoms" might be established in the *"New Heaven"* or upon the *"New Earth"*. I don't completely understand these terms so I can't say for certain. We do know from Scripture that these Kingdoms will last forever, (Rev. 22:5), and that God and Christ will dwell amongst His people during them, (Rev. 21:3). But even the earliest Christians realized that our Lord's Kingdom was of a Spiritual rather than earthly nature. Jesus Himself said:

"... The kingdom of God cometh not with observation: Neither shall they say, Lo here! Or, lo there! For, behold, the kingdom of God is within you." (Luke 17:20-21)

Our Lord's Kingdom is established in love, grace, and truth and its foundation is set in our hearts, minds, and souls, (II Cor. 3:2-3). John baptized with water. But the One who comes after him, the One whose shoe latchet he was unworthy to loosen, baptizes with fire and the Holy Spirit, (Luke 3:16-17). With fire because fire cleanses and purifies all things. With the Holy Spirit to teach us truth and how to live our new lives in Christ. When Christ comes and we are taken to be with Him in His Kingdom we will never see sadness nor corruption again. Christ's Kingdom is an everlasting Kingdom but the millennium is not.

Like I said before, I can't be sure where or how these "Everlasting Kingdoms" will be instituted. There's not enough evidence provided in Scripture to make a well-founded conclusion. But I am sure they will not be fulfilled in the millennial reign upon this planet. In fact, if one takes a close look at Rev. 20, he will notice that nothing is expressly stated therein about an earthly reign. If my readers would like to review this matter further, I have a few books at my disposal that might prove helpful: *American Saints and Seers*, by Edward Price, *Religion in the Twentieth Century*, by Vergillius Ferm, and W. Arndt provides an excellent 8-point rebuttal against an earthly millennial reign in his book entitled, *Fundamental Christian Beliefs*, pp. 88-90. These are just a few books in my possession. There are many more books in your local library that address this subject

I will close this chapter with these words:

"How can this (Rev. 20) bear any kind of literal interpretation? Satan is bound a thousand years, and the earth is in peace; righteousness flourishes, and Jesus Christ alone reigns. This state of things may continue forever if the imprisonment of Satan be continued. Satan, however, is loosed at the end of the thousand years, and goes out and deceives the nations, and peace is banished from the face of the earth, and a most dreadful war takes place, etc. These can be only symbolical representations, utterly incapable of the sense generally put upon them." (Clarke's Commentary; Vol. 6, page 1,056).

CHAPTER THIRTEEN

THE BATTLE WITH GOG AND MAGOG

This portion of my inquisition is somewhat tangential. The evidence I'm about to advance right now does not confute the millennium directly. But anything that casts doubt on this concept is beneficial to my argument. It is this evidence which initially forced me to realize that I was mistaken concerning symbolical prophecy in general, and more specifically my views regarding the millennial reign. Hopefully the same effect can be achieved with some of my readers.

After the millennium Satan is released from his prison and he sets out to deceive the nations of the earth. His efforts culminate in a fearful battle with Gog and Magog:

"And when the thousand years are expired, Satan shall be loosed out of his prison, And shall go out to deceive the nations which are in the four quarters of the earth, Gog and Magog, to gather them together to battle: the number of whom is as the sand of the sea. And they went up on the breadth of the earth, and compassed the camp of the saints about, and the beloved city: and fire came down from God out of heaven, and devoured them." (Rev. 20:7-9)

There is one observation I'd like to make before continuing. The word *"saints"* in this passage doesn't fundamentally mean "resurrected holy ones" as some people might mistake it for. When we think of the way this word is used today we think of individuals who have been elevated to the status of sainthood after they have passed away. But that is not the way this word was applied in the New Testament. The original Greek word used here is *"hagios"* which means "set apart" (Young 831). This term is commonly employed in the Bible and designates God's elect and all believers in general:

"For it hath pleased them of Macedonia and Achaia to make a certain contribution __for the poor saints which are at Jerusalem.__" (Rom. 15:26)

This was a popular expression in the Bible. Those who are still confused about this word's original meaning and application might want to consult the following list of examples for further references: (Acts 9:13, 32, 41; 26:10; Rom. 1:7; 12:13; 15:25, 26, 31; 16:2, 15; I Cor. 1:2; 14:33; 16:1, 15; II Cor. 1:1; 8:4; 9:1, 12; 13:13; Eph. 1:1, 15, 18; 2:19; 3:8, 18; 4:12; 5:3; Phil. 1:1; 4:21, 22; Col. 1:2, 4, 12, 26; I Tim. 5:10; Philemon 5, 7; Heb. 13:24; Jude 3). I am making this distinction now to show that Gog here is not necessarily attacking those who were reigning for the millennium. This battle is enjoined by *"the nations which are in the four quarters of the earth"*.

Concerning Gog and Magog: A very similar conflict with these entities is portrayed in the prophecies of Ezekiel, Chapters 38 and 39. Not only do these two confrontations appear analogous, but I have discovered an abundance of evidence to corroborate a very convincing theory that these two Gogs are actually one and the same. It is quite noteworthy that a great battle with Gog is mentioned at **no other place** in Scripture. That's some coincidence.

If I can show that these two Gogs are more alike than different, the theories of many millennium proponents will be called into question. If I can show that these entities are **probably** identical, many advocates of the millennium will be forced to seriously alter their views. The reason is this: Many chiliasts have openly declared that Ezekiel's Gog represents Russia and its massive military thrust into the oil-rich countries of the Middle East. Actually there is a significant amount of evidence to support this idea. Naturally, however, that cannot be established as fact although many individuals irresponsibly treat it as such. There are a large number of books on the market dealing with this topic. The most famous one has got to be Hal Lindsey's *The Late Great Planet Earth*. This book has sold something like ten million copies. Tim LaHaye borrows extensively from his work as well.

It is not my intention to refute the idea that Ezekiel's Gog represents Russia. I personally don't care much one way or the other. The important thing is that these people do say that it represents Russia. They've left no room for error in this respect and that was a big mistake. These people are claiming that Revelation's Gog represents something entirely different. Some of these people fail to even mention Gog when discussing the millennium. But the ones who do often insert substitute phrases for these terms, eg. "the rebellious nations", "the evil human countries", etc. How can these people completely overlook and ignore the striking resemblances between these two Gogs? The answer is obvious: According to their theories, the conflict with Ezekiel's Gog (Russia) is to take place very soon. But the conflict with Revelation's Gog takes place **after the millennium**.

The problem is apparent: These people believe the millennium will take place upon this planet. There has never been a time in recorded history when Christ personally reigned upon this Earth for a thousand years. Hence, they conclude that this phenomenon is yet to occur. And because they've reached that conclusion they postulate that there are no correlations between these two entities. On the contrary, however, there are an astronomical amount of correlations between them. You see, I used to overlook these "small phrases" too. So I know how it is. You can bet the farm that if Revelation's Gog didn't follow the millennium these individuals could easily draw the correlative lines between them. They've ran into this roadblock and if they're anything like I was, this has been a thorn in their side ever since they first sat down and read it. If that were not true, then why haven't they addressed this question directly? These people have meticulously explained every little detail about the millennium. Since they've made such a comprehensive study of this subject, why haven't they endeavored to distinguish just who Revelation's Gog is referring to? I'll tell you why: Because they will invariably be faced with the prospect that these two Gogs might be the same. And since this would destroy their complex and well-founded theories about Ezekiel's Gog they choose to simply ignore Revelation's Gog. Because if Ezekiel's Gog represents the Russian invasion of the Middle East and this confrontation takes place after the millennium, then the millennium must have occurred already. The only other alternative would be to admit that Ezekiel's Gog might not represent the Russian invasion after all. All of the arguments used by these people to substantiate their theory about Ezekiel's Gog can also be used on Revelation's Gog, with one huge exception: The battle with Revelation's Gog transpires **after** the millennium.

I will now delineate eight major similarities between these two mysterious figures. Remember, I do not intend to prove they are twins. I don't have to. All I have to prove is that they could be.

8 SIMILARITIES OF REVELATION'S GOG & EZEKIEL'S GOG

Their names are identical. There is no other place in the Bible where a great battle is fought against Gog and Magog except in Rev. 20 and Ezekiel 38 and 39.

This confrontation occurs at or near the end of time in both prophecies: (Eze. 38:8, 16; Rev. 20:11; Rev. 21:1).

A resurrection is mentioned prior to this conflict in both prophecies: (Eze. 37:1-28; Rev. 20:4-6).

Both Gogs possess a multitudinous military personnel: (Eze. 38:4-6, 9, 15, 22; Eze. 39:4; Rev. 20:9).

Both Gogs attack the Holy Land: (Eze. 38:8, 14, 16, 18; Eze. 39:4, 11; Rev. 20:9).

Both Gogs are destroyed in the same manner, by fire and brimstone coming down from God: (Eze. 38:22; Eze. 39:6; Rev. 20:9).

Both Gogs are destroyed for the same reason, for attacking Israel: (Eze. 38:16, 18-19; Eze. 39:1-4; Rev. 20:9).

The vision of the Heavenly temple, (Eze. 40-48), and the vision of the new Heaven and Earth and new Jerusalem, (Rev. 21-22). If one examines these two visions comparatively, he will notice an abundance of interrelations which is rather astonishing. Here's a few examples:
- Ezekiel 40:3 with Revelation 21:15
- Ezekiel 43:7 with Revelation 21:3
- Ezekiel 47:1 with Revelation 22:1
- Ezekiel 47:7, 12 with Revelation 22:2
- Ezekiel 48 with Revelation 21:10-14

- Ezekiel 48:31 with Revelation 21:12
- Ezekiel 48:31-34 with Revelation 21:13
- Ezekiel 48:35 with Revelation 21:3
- Ezekiel 48:35 with Revelation 22:3

I have two additional reasons why I think these two characters may be the same: The Targums of Jonathan ben Uzziel and the Jerusalem Targum. Targums were translations of the Bible made in ancient Israel into vernacular tongues for the benefit of those who didn't understand the original correctly. These Targums are of special critical value and to dispute their importance is irresponsible. These Targums were made from the original Holy Scriptures. They will help us to better understand the manner in which the Holy Bible was interpreted and understood around the time of Christ. They will also show that Ezekiel's Gog and Revelation's Gog are practically inseparable.

The Targum of Jonathan ben Uzziel: "Behold, a king shall come up from the land of Magog (Eze. 38:2; Eze. 39:6; Rev. 20:8) in the last days (Eze. 38:8, 16; Rev. 20:11; Rev. 21:1) and shall gather the kings together (Eze. 38:5-6; Rev. 20:8), and the leaders clothed with armor (Eze. 38:4), and all people shall obey him: and they shall wage war in the land of Israel (Eze. 38:8, 16, 18; Eze. 39:2, 4; Rev. 20:9) against the children of the captivity (Eze. 39:23), but the hour of lamentation has long been prepared for them, for they shall be slain by the flame of fire which shall proceed from under the throne of glory (Eze. 38:18-22; Eze. 39:6; Rev. 20:9), and their dead carcasses shall fall on the mountains of Israel (Eze. 39:4); and all the wild beasts of the field, and the wild fowl of heaven shall come and devour their dead carcasses (Eze. 39:4, 17-21); and afterwards all the dead of Israel shall rise again to life (Rev. 20:11-13), and shall enjoy the delights prepared for them from the beginning, and shall receive the reward of their works (Rev. 20:13)."

The Jerusalem Targum: "In the very end of time (Eze. 38:8, 16; Rev. 20:11; Rev. 21:1) Gog and Magog (Eze. 38:2, 3, 14, 16, 18; Eze. 39:1, 6, 11; Rev. 20:8) shall come up against Jerusalem (Eze. 38:18; Rev. 20:9) and they shall fall by the hand of the King Messiah;

169

and for seven whole years shall the children of Israel light their fires with the wood of their war-like engines (Eze. 39:9), and they shall not go to the wood nor cut down any tree (Eze. 39:10)."

(Targums taken from Clarke's Commentary; Vol. 6, page 1,056). These observations are overwhelming. They cannot be ignored. I have definitely proven that these two Gogs could very easily be one and the same. Who could possibly deny this? How could it be that the millennium is yet to transpire if these two Gogs are the same? According to Hal Lindsey and Tim LaHaye among others, the conflict with Ezekiel's Gog is supposed to take place very soon, not a thousand years from now. According to The Global 2,000 Report there won't even be any oil left in the Mideast by then. We'll be fortunate if it lasts for a hundred years. On the other hand, if this battle is to occur after the millennium, Gog may not represent the Russian invasion after all.

To agree that these two entities **might** be identical is enough to call the integrity of both of these theories into question and places both of them in serious contention. These two ideas oppose each other like opposite ends of a magnet, yet collide headlong into one another when considered in this light. Like I said before, I'm not saying these two figures are actually twins. But as long as they could be we must treat them respectively. With all the correlations I've delineated who can say these two characters definitely are not the same? Nobody.

CHAPTER FOURTEEN

CLOSING NOTES ON THE MILLENNIUM

I've shown that this earth will be pulverized at Christ's Second Advent. Thus, the millennium could not transpire at that time. I've also shown that our Lord's Second Coming/ the last judgment/ the rapture of Christ's elect/ the resurrection/ and the end of the world are all one and the same event. There is not a thousand-year period between any two of those events: (Chapter Nine). I've portrayed the extreme risk of false christs with the millennial concept. I've shown that Jesus Christ will never reappear upon this earth in the form of a man again: (Chapter Ten). I've shown that it is dangerous and self-condemning to tamper with the apocalypse so as to change or alter its message(s) or meaning(s). I've shown how it is a mistake to believe in any manmade concept that has been fabricated from symbolical prophecy. I've shown how it is preposterous to declare guesses to be absolute fact. I've shown that there are many more ways than one to look at, consider, and interpret the Book of Revelation. I've advanced an alternative mode of interpretation for Rev. 20: (Chapter Eleven). I've shown that many of the Old Testament prophecies that are pointed out as the millennium couldn't possibly pertain to it because they are said to last forever. I've also shown that this earth will not last forever. Therefore, these "Everlasting Kingdoms" could not possibly occur upon this planet. I've shown that there is nothing mentioned in Rev. 20 about a reign on this earth. I've shown that Christ's Kingdom is Spiritual, not earthly, in nature: (Chapter Twelve). I've delineated the numerous close comparisons between Ezekiel's Gog and Revelation's Gog. I've shown that if it is at all possible these two figures are twins, then the theories of many chiliasts will be found to be in serious error: (Chapter Thirteen).

If that isn't enough to convince a person that the millennium is a fallacious concept, then he must be one stubborn individual. There's nothing more I can do. I don't know what else to say. If one is harboring the slightest doubt about this conception, why continue to believe in it wholeheartedly? And like I said before, if there is an element of danger associated with this, how can it possibly be the truth?

The millennium could easily be a "stumbling block" to the Christian community. It could create a great barrier to divide them against one another. After all, what better barrier could there be to divide Christianity than the emergence of a false christ? Sin and temptation will pullulate in the mind of the scholar and unbeliever alike. It could quickly grow to be greater than the mountains. Both the scholar, as well as the unbeliever, will have to decide immediately what side of the proverbial fence to leap on. There's only two sides and it's impossible to balance in the middle. It's either all the way or not at all when it comes to false christs. Heed the words of our Lord:

"Every kingdom divided against itself is brought to desolation: and a house divided against a house falleth." *(Luke 11:17)*

And if a false christ succeeds in dividing Christians, how then can Christianity stand? Why did Christ say?:

"...Nevertheless when the Son of man cometh, shall he find faith on the earth?" *(Luke 18:8)*

The rapture and millennial theories have practically become axioms in many religious circles. In too many Churches these concepts have been included in their creed of faith! Don't these people realize what they've done? They have built the infrastructure of their faith on manmade concepts. Yea, they've built their Church on the sand. And when the whirlwind of the wrath of God blows upon it and the rains beat down relentlessly, how can it possibly stand?

Friends and neighbors, I beseech you, separate yourselves from these manmade concepts. The only important things are God the Father, Jesus Christ our Lord and Savior, and the Holy Spirit. Only these are worthy of unfaltering belief. Any view, concept, theory, opinion, etc. which could potentially divide Christianity should be discarded without hesitation. If there are good Christians on both sides of the issue, how can the issue be more important than the

Spiritual unity it sacrifices?

After reading the Holy Bible for myself I realized and understood that the rapture and the millennium were nothing but chimerical fables. But when I embarked upon this arduous mission of confuting those two theories, I found that I was dealing with a problem that is nearly without solution. I found that if I inadvertently omitted one single thing, the proponents of these concepts would probably capitalize upon it with much criticism. These ideas have been inveterated over an expansive period of time and I feel helpless in this attempt to deracinate them. But as David slew Goliath, it is my only hope that God will assist me in this venture.

I've been told, by some, that I have no business writing this book. They say that since I have no college degrees or other reputable credentials, then I cannot possibly know what I'm talking about. Doesn't the book speak for itself? And if I don't write it, who will? God uses the young and ignorant to confound the old and wise, and base things of the world, and things which are not, to bring to nought things which are. So no flesh should glory in God's sight and claim to have learned these things on their own, (I Cor. 1:26-31). What? Should I claim to have learned these things on my own? Or should I give to the Lord what is His? Is it possible for a man to learn these truths without the assistance of the Holy Spirit? Heretofore this has only been a vexation to understand:

"From the time that it goeth forth it shall take you: for morning by morning shall it pass over, by day and by night: and it shall be a vexation only to understand the report." (Isa. 28:19).

That passage has haunted me for many years. But now a feeling of great peace has overcome me. This is not a feeling I'm accustomed to. I realize this book has finally come to maturity. It will be published whether I live or die.

The rapture and the millennium are, as my good friend Jeff once said, "Brothers of Deception". They are up to their necks in an ocean of deceit. It is my hope that this inquest shoves them into the depths and they drown in their own lies.

Works Consulted

Phillips, J.B. *Letters to Young Churches*. New York: MacMillan Co., 1960.

Young, Robert LL D. *Analytical Concordance of the Bible*. Nashville: Thomas Nelson Inc., 1982.